EASY
CURRIES

EASY
CURRIES

Jody Vassallo

photographs by Deirdre Rooney

HACHETTE Illustrated

introduction

I have been travelling to Thailand and enjoying its cuisine for the past 20 years, so I was overjoyed when I was asked to write a book on Thai and Indian curries. More recently, I embarked on a journey to India with one mission – to unravel the mystery behind the myriad spices that form the foundation of Indian cuisine. The recipes in this book echo the amazing tastes and flavours I have encountered over the years. They are quick, easy and accessible to most palates – if you find you like a little more heat, experiment by adding extra chilli powder or curry paste. Making your own curry paste makes the world of difference (and recipes are provided at the back of the book), but there are also plenty of good-quality readymade pastes available. I hope you enjoy making and eating these recipes as much as I have.

ingredients

mace

cloves

thai basil leaves

paneer

galangal

kaffir limes

kaffir lime leaves

black mustard seeds

tamarind

cardamom pods

dried red chillies

asafoetida

ingredients

shrimp paste

small green chillies

curry leaves

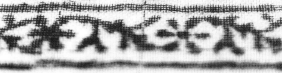

shaved palm sugar

ghee

asian shallots

fenugreek seeds

red onion

thai fish sauce

large green chillies

lemongrass

saffron

chicken and duck

12

duck and pineapple curry

If you cannot find ripe fresh pineapple for this recipe, use canned. If Chinese duck is not available, you can roast duck breasts on the bone and then chop them into three. You would need 4–6 breasts for this recipe.

Preparation time: 15 minutes,
cooking time: 25 minutes, serves 4–6

400 ml/14 fl oz can coconut cream
2–4 tablespoons red curry paste
250 ml/9 fl oz/1 cup chicken stock
2 stalks lemongrass, bruised with the back
of a large knife
1 Chinese roast duck, cut into bite-size pieces
4 spring onions (scallions), sliced
3 kaffir lime leaves, shredded
2 tomatoes, chopped
400 g/14 oz fresh pineapple, cut into
bite-size pieces
2 tablespoons chopped fresh coriander
(cilantro), to serve

Put the coconut cream into a wok, add the curry paste and cook, stirring occasionally, for 5 minutes, or until the oil starts to separate from the cream and the paste is fragrant.

Add the stock, lemongrass, duck, spring onions, lime leaves, tomatoes and pineapple and bring to the boil. Reduce the heat and simmer, uncovered, for 15 minutes. Serve topped with the coriander.

kerala chicken stew

Kerala is a region in the south of India and its name means 'land of the coconut'. Indeed, most people in the south use coconut oil to cook in and also often enrich their curries with coconut milk.

Preparation time: 15 minutes,
cooking time: 45 minutes, serves 4–6

2 tablespoons vegetable oil
½ teaspoon fenugreek seeds
1 cinnamon stick
1 teaspoon cardamom pods, bruised
2 small green chillies, sliced in half
½ teaspoon turmeric
12 curry leaves
1 red onion, sliced
1 kg/2 lb 4 oz chicken thigh fillets, cut into thick strips
12 baby potatoes
2 carrots, sliced
1 green pepper (bell pepper), sliced
400 ml/14 fl oz/1¾ cups coconut milk
½ teaspoon salt
1 teaspoon grated palm sugar or brown sugar

Heat the oil in a large pan, add the fenugreek seeds and cook them over a medium heat for 3 minutes, or until they brown and pop.

Next add the cinnamon, cardamom, chillies, turmeric, curry leaves and onion and cook for 5 minutes, or until the onion is soft and golden.

Add the chicken to the pan and cook it for 5 minutes, or until it is browned. Add the potatoes, carrots, green pepper, coconut milk, salt and sugar and bring the mixture to the boil. Reduce the heat and simmer, covered, for 15 minutes. Remove the lid and simmer uncovered for a further 15 minutes, or until the oil separates from the coconut milk.

chicken pistachio

Try to find fresh bright green pistachios, as they will give this dish a vibrant green colour. This is a reasonably mild curry, so if you want something spicier increase the amount of chillies used.

Preparation time: 25 minutes,
cooking time: 1 hour, serves 4–6

150 g/5½ oz/1 generous cup pistachio kernels
2 small green chillies
3 tablespoons chopped fresh coriander (cilantro)
3 tablespoons vegetable oil
750 g/1 lb 10 oz chicken thigh fillets, cubed
1 onion, chopped
1 tablespoon grated fresh ginger
3 garlic cloves, chopped
1 tablespoon garam masala
250 ml/9 fl oz/1 cup chicken stock
½ teaspoon salt
125 ml/4 fl oz/½ cup cream

Put the pistachios into a pan, cover them with water and bring to the boil. Cook them for 10 minutes, then drain and cool. Rub the nuts in a dry tea towel to remove the skins.

Put the pistachios, chillies and coriander into a food processor and process to form a paste. Heat the oil in a large pan, add the chicken and cook it over a medium heat for 5 minutes, or until it is browned, then remove it.

Place the onion in the pan and cook it over a medium heat for 10 minutes, or until it is golden brown. Add the ginger and garlic and cook for 2 minutes. Add the garam masala and cook for 3 minutes, or until fragrant.

Return the chicken to the pan, and add the pistachio mixture, chicken stock, salt and cream. Simmer for 30 minutes, or until the chicken is tender.

kerala chicken stew

chicken pistachio

jungle chicken curry

This curry does not use coconut milk like other Thai-style curries. If you like the sound of the dish but don't want the spice, simply reduce the amount of curry paste you use.

Preparation time: 15 minutes,
cooking time: 15 minutes, serves 4—6

2 teaspoons vegetable oil
1—2 tablespoons jungle curry paste or green curry paste
2 tablespoons Thai fish sauce
500 g/1 lb 2 oz chicken thigh fillets, sliced
500 ml/18 fl oz/2 cups chicken stock
200 g/7 oz can bamboo shoots, drained
200 g/7 oz fresh or canned baby corn
100 g/3½ oz pea aubergine (pea eggplant)
3 kaffir lime leaves, torn
1 teaspoon grated palm sugar or brown sugar

Heat the oil in a wok, add the curry paste and cook over a medium heat for 3 minutes, or until the curry paste is fragrant.

Add the fish sauce and chicken and cook for 5 minutes, or until the chicken starts to brown. Add the stock, bamboo shoots, baby corn, aubergine and lime leaves, then bring the mixture to the boil, reduce the heat and simmer for 5 minutes, or until the chicken is cooked. Finally, season the dish with sugar.

mango chicken

This recipe is one of many that use tamarind concentrate – this can be bought in Asian food stores or made by soaking tamarind pulp in boiling water until soft, then pressing it through a sieve (strainer) to extract the juice.

Preparation time: 15 minutes,
cooking time: 40 minutes, serves 4–6

2 tablespoons vegetable oil
1 red onion, sliced
3 dried large red chillies
1 teaspoon garam masala
½ teaspoon turmeric
500 g/1 lb 2 oz chicken thigh fillets, cut into thick strips
400 ml/14 fl oz/1¾ cups coconut milk
2 ripe mangoes, peeled and cut into thick slices
2 teaspoons tamarind concentrate
½ teaspoon salt
2 tablespoons fresh coriander (cilantro) leaves, to serve
½ small red onion, sliced, to serve

Heat the oil in a pan, add the onion and cook it over a medium heat for 10 minutes, or until it is golden brown. Add the chillies, garam masala and turmeric and cook for 2 minutes, or until fragrant.

Add the chicken to the pan and cook it for 5 minutes, or until browned. Stir in the coconut milk, mangoes, tamarind and salt. Bring the mixture to the boil, then reduce the heat and simmer it, uncovered, for 20 minutes, or until the chicken is tender. Serve the dish sprinkled with the coriander and onion. (The red chillies can be removed before serving if you prefer.)

thai chicken curry

The kaffir lime leaves impart a unique fragrant lime flavour in this recipe. If you cannot find them, look for dried ones in an Asian food store and reconstitute them in hot water. Create your own curry paste here, as it will make a huge difference.

Preparation time: 15 minutes,
cooking time: 20 minutes, serves 4

1 tablespoon vegetable oil
500 g/1 lb 2 oz chicken thigh fillets, sliced
1–2 tablespoons green curry paste
400 ml/14 fl oz/1¾ cups coconut milk
4 kaffir lime leaves, shredded
200 g/7 oz green beans, sliced
200 g/7 oz can bamboo shoots, drained
2 tablespoons Thai fish sauce
2 tablespoons grated palm sugar or brown sugar
20 g/¾ oz/⅓ cup fresh coriander (cilantro) leaves, to serve

Heat the oil in a wok, add the chicken and stir-fry it over a medium-high heat for 5 minutes, or until browned. Add the curry paste and stir-fry for 3 minutes, until fragrant.

Stir in the coconut milk and lime leaves and bring the mixture to the boil. Reduce the heat to a simmer, add the beans and bamboo shoots and simmer for 5 minutes, or until the beans are tender.

Season the dish with the fish sauce and sugar. Serve it topped with the coriander leaves.

duck with lychees

Lychees are one of my all-time favourite fruits and they work so well to cut through the richness of the duck in this recipe. Of course if you can get your hands on fresh lychees, do use them in this recipe.

Preparation time: 25–30 minutes + 10 minutes
soaking, cooking time: 20 minutes, serves 4–6

2 thin aubergines (eggplants), sliced
1 Chinese roast duck
500 ml/18 fl oz/generous 2 cups coconut milk
1–2 tablespoons red curry paste
4 kaffir lime leaves
400 g/14 oz can lychees, drained
2 tablespoons Thai fish sauce
1 tablespoon grated palm sugar or brown sugar
2 tablespoons fresh Thai basil leaves or coriander (cilantro) leaves, to serve
1 large red chilli, seeded and thinly sliced, to serve

Soak the aubergine slices in cold salted water for 10 minutes, then drain. Meanwhile, cut the duck into bite-size pieces, using a large cleaver or sharp knife.

Heat the coconut milk in a wok, add the curry paste and cook for 10 minutes, or until the oil starts to separate from the coconut. (Stir the mixture occasionally to prevent it from sticking to the bottom of the wok.)

Add the duck, lime leaves, lychees, aubergine, fish sauce and sugar, bring the dish to the boil, reduce the heat and simmer for 10 minutes. Serve the dish topped with the basil and thinly sliced chillies.

thai chicken curry

duck with lychees

tangy chicken and mango stir-fry

I developed this recipe after spending time at my sister's home in Cairns, Australia. In her backyard she had a huge mango tree and each morning the lawn was carpeted with mangoes. I couldn't bear to throw any away, so I put mango in everything I cooked!

Preparation time: 10 minutes,
cooking time: 20 minutes, serves 4–6

1 tablespoon vegetable oil
1–2 tablespoons red curry paste
500 g/1 lb 2 oz chicken breast fillets, sliced
4 spring onions (scallions) cut into
5 cm/2 inch pieces
125 ml/4 fl oz/½ cup chicken stock
250 ml/9 fl oz/1 cup coconut milk
6 kaffir lime leaves, finely shredded
230 g/8¼ oz can water chestnuts, drained
2 firm mangoes, cut into thick slices
1 tablespoon Thai fish sauce
1 tablespoon lime juice
2 tablespoons fresh coriander (cilantro)
leaves, to serve

Heat the oil in a wok, add the curry paste and cook over a medium heat for 3–5 minutes, or until the paste starts to separate from the oil and become fragrant. Add the chicken breast fillets and spring onions and cook for 5 minutes, or until the fillets start to brown.

Add the stock, coconut milk, lime leaves, water chestnuts and mangoes, bring the mixture to the boil, then reduce the heat and simmer for 5 minutes, or until the chicken is tender.

Season with the fish sauce and lime juice, then serve the dish topped with the coriander leaves.

mulligatawny chicken soup

This soup was first created for the British in India. Mulligatawny is a combination of two Tamil words, which, roughly translated, mean 'pepper water'. The soup itself is much more appetizing than the name suggests!

Preparation time: 20 minutes, cooking time: 40 minutes, serves 4–6

2 tablespoons vegetable oil
1 tablespoon garam masala
500 g/1 lb 2 oz chicken thigh fillets, thinly sliced
1 onion, thinly sliced
2 teaspoons grated fresh ginger
1 garlic clove, chopped
½ teaspoon fennel seeds
½ teaspoon turmeric
1 cinnamon stick
1 small green chilli, seeded and sliced
1 litre/32 fl oz/4 cups chicken stock
400 ml/14 fl oz/1¾ cups coconut milk
3 ripe, medium-sized tomatoes

Heat the oil in a large pan, add the garam masala and cook over a medium heat for 3 minutes, or until fragrant.

Add the chicken to the pan and cook it for 5 minutes, or until it starts to brown. Add the onion, ginger, garlic, fennel, turmeric, cinnamon stick, chilli, stock, coconut milk and tomatoes and simmer for 30 minutes, or until the chicken is tender.

chicken and duck

chicken tikka bites

Chicken tikka is normally cooked in a tandoor oven, but at home you can use the oven, grill (broiler) or a covered barbecue (grill). These bites are nice served as nibbles for a cocktail party – serve them with cocktail sticks (toothpicks).

Preparation time: 10 minutes + 4 hours marinating, cooking time: 15 minutes, serves 6–8

4 tablespoons tandoori paste
1 tablespoon lemon juice
4 tablespoons grated fresh ginger
4 garlic cloves, chopped
250 g/9 oz/1 cup natural (plain) yoghurt
1 kg/2 lb 4 oz chicken thigh fillets, cut into bite-size pieces
naan bread or poppadom and cucumber raita, to serve

Combine the tandoori paste, lemon juice, ginger, garlic and yoghurt. Add the chicken to the marinade, cover and refrigerate it for a minimum of 4 hours or, if possible, overnight.

Cook the chicken under a preheated grill (broiler) set on a medium-high heat for 15 minutes, turning it several times during the cooking process until tender. Serve the chicken with rounds of naan or poppadom and some cucumber raita (see page 156).

butter chicken

This very popular Indian dish was a challenge to replicate at home, but I am more than happy with the end result. To keep things simple, I have used a readymade tandoori paste and grilled (broiled) the chicken, then added it to the sauce.

Preparation time: 15 minutes, cooking time: 30 minutes, serves 4–6

1 kg/2 lb 4 oz chicken thigh fillets, cut into bite-size pieces
3 tablespoons tandoori paste
125 g/4½ oz/½ cup natural (plain) yoghurt
800 g/1 lb 12 oz can chopped tomatoes
1 teaspoon garam masala
½ teaspoon paprika
250 ml/9 fl oz/1 cup single (light) cream
2 tablespoons grated palm sugar or brown sugar
50 g/1¾ oz chilled ghee or clarified butter
½ teaspoon salt

Put the chicken into a bowl, add the tandoori paste and yoghurt and mix well to coat the chicken in the tandoori mixture. Arrange the chicken in shallow baking dish and cook under a preheated grill (broiler) set on a high heat until tender. Remove the chicken and set it aside.

Pour the juices from the baking dish into a pan, add the tomatoes, garam masala, paprika, cream and sugar. Bring the mixture to the boil and cook it over a high heat for 10 minutes, or until the sauce is thick and creamy. Add the chicken, ghee and salt and simmer for 3 minutes, or until the ghee melts and the chicken is heated through.

chicken tikka bites

butter chicken

simple chicken curry

This is a basic formula for a simple curry. However, you can process the onion, garlic and ginger into a smooth paste first, as is traditional with most north Indian curries. This will provide a fuller, more potent flavour base.

Preparation time: 15 minutes, cooking time: 1 hour, serves 4–6

3 tablespoons vegetable oil
1 red onion, chopped
2 garlic cloves, chopped
1 tablespoon chopped fresh ginger
2 teaspoons ground coriander
½ teaspoon ground cumin
½ teaspoon garam masala
½ teaspoon hot chilli powder
½ teaspoon turmeric
500 g/1 lb 2 oz chicken thigh fillets, cut into bite-size pieces
400 g/14 oz can chopped tomatoes
125 ml/4 fl oz/½ cup chicken stock
250 ml/9 fl oz/1 cup coconut milk
½ teaspoon salt

Heat the oil in a pan, then add the onion and cook it over a medium heat for 15 minutes or until it is golden brown. Add the garlic and ginger and cook for a further 5 minutes.

Add all the spices to the pan and cook them for 3 minutes, or until fragrant. Add the chicken pieces and cook it for 5 minutes, or until browned. Stir in the tomatoes, stock, coconut milk and salt. Bring the mixture to the boil, reduce the heat and simmer it, covered, for 15 minutes. Remove the lid and cook, uncovered, for a further 15 minutes, or until the chicken is tender and the oil has separated from the sauce.

satay chicken curry

Satay is a very popular flavouring in Thailand and dishes made with it can range from being very spicy to mild and sweet. You can also try substituting the chicken with prawns (shrimp) for a tasty alternative.

Preparation time: 15 minutes, cooking time: 20 minutes, serves 4

1 tablespoon vegetable oil
2 tablespoons red curry paste
2 tablespoons peanut butter
500 g/1 lb 2 oz chicken breast fillets, chopped into cubes
400 ml/14 fl oz/1¾ cups coconut milk
200 g/7 oz broccoli florets
1 red pepper (bell pepper), sliced
1 carrot, sliced
100 g/3½ oz green beans, sliced
1 tablespoon Thai fish sauce
1 tablespoon grated palm sugar or brown sugar
3 tablespoons roughly chopped peanuts, to serve
1 large red chilli, seeded and thinly sliced, to serve
3 tablespoons roughly chopped fresh coriander (cilantro), to serve

Heat the oil in a wok, add the curry paste and peanut butter and cook over a medium heat for 5 minutes, or until the oil starts to separate from the paste.

Add the chicken to the wok and stir-fry for 5 minutes, or until browned. Next add the coconut milk, vegetables, fish sauce and palm sugar, bring the mixture to the boil, reduce the heat and simmer for 10 minutes.

Serve the dish topped with the chopped nuts, chilli and coriander.

chicken dopiaza

Dopiaza means two onions, and this dish uses onions in two ways – fried and then simmered. Onions are widely used in Indian cooking, but generally you will see only red onions – try to find small, sweet ones too for this dish.

Preparation time: 15 minutes,
cooking time: 1 hour, serves 6–8

2 tablespoons vegetable oil
2 red onions, sliced into rings (to serve)
1 teaspoon green cardamom pods, bruised
1 teaspoon cloves
3 large, dried red chillies
2 bay leaves
2 tablespoons grated fresh ginger
½ teaspoon turmeric
1 kg/2 lb 4 oz chicken drumsticks, scored in the thickest part
6 pickling onions
375 ml/13 fl oz/generous 1½ cups chicken stock
125 g/4½ oz/½ cup natural (plain) yoghurt

Heat the oil in a pan, add the red onions and cook over a medium heat for 10 minutes, or until the onions are golden brown and caramelized. Remove them from the pan and drain them on absorbent kitchen paper.

Add the spices to the oil and cook them for 5 minutes, or until browned. Add the drumsticks, pickling onions and stock and bring the pan to the boil, then reduce the heat and simmer for 30 minutes. Finally add the yoghurt and simmer, uncovered, for 15 minutes, or until the chicken is tender. Serve topped with the fried onions. (The chillies can be removed before serving if you prefer.)

chicken and duck

mustard tomato chicken

This dish is inspired by the flavours of the south – mustard seeds and curry leaves. I have added tomatoes and sugar to create a sweet spicy dish that is delicious served with lemon rice (see page 156).

Preparation time: 15 minutes,
cooking time: 1 hour 10 minutes, serves 4–6

2 tablespoons vegetable oil
1 tablespoon black mustard seeds
1 red onion, sliced
1 kg/2 lb 4 oz chicken pieces, scored in the thickest part
10 curry leaves
1 teaspoon hot chilli powder
400 g/14 oz can chopped tomatoes
100 g/3½ oz fresh pitted dates, halved
2 tablespoons white vinegar
55 g/2 oz/generous ¼ cup grated palm sugar or brown sugar
1 teaspoon garam masala

Heat the oil in a large pan, add the mustard seeds and cook them over a medium heat for 3 minutes, or until they begin to pop.

Add the onion and cook, stirring regularly, for 10 minutes or until golden. Add the chicken pieces in small batches, cooking them for 5 minutes, or until golden brown, and setting the cooked pieces aside until all are cooked.

Put all the chicken back in the pan, then add the curry leaves and chilli powder and cook for 3 minutes. Stir in the tomatoes, dates vinegar, sugar and garam masala, then cover and cook for 30 minutes.

Remove the lid and cook for a further 15 minutes, or until the chicken is tender and the sauce is thick.

cashew chicken

Cashews are frequently used in Indian recipes and, as in most places in the world, they are quite an expensive luxury. However, Indians are able to select between high quality and lower quality and purchase according to their budget.

Preparation time: 30 minutes + 15 minutes
soaking + 4 hours marinating, cooking time:
1 hour, serves 4–6

4 chicken breasts on the bone
3 tablespoons ginger garlic paste (see page 152)
125 g/4½ oz/½ cup natural (plain) yoghurt
1 teaspoon hot chilli powder
1 teaspoon garam masala
½ teaspoon salt
150 g/5½ oz/1 cup cashews
3 red onions, chopped
3 tablespoons vegetable oil
1 bay leaf
3 green cardamom pods, bruised
250 ml/9 fl oz/1 generous cup single (light) cream
fresh coriander (cilantro) leaves, to serve

Cut the chicken breasts in half through the middle, put them into a bowl and add the ginger garlic paste, yoghurt, chilli, garam masala and salt. Cover and allow to marinate for a minimum of 4 hours – preferably overnight.

Soak the cashews in 60 ml/2 fl oz/¼ cup of hot water for 15 minutes, or until soft, then transfer them to a food processor or spice grinder and process to form a smooth paste. Remove them and then put the chopped onions into the food processor and process until smooth.

Heat the oil in a pan, add the bay leaf and cardamom and cook for 2 minutes, or until the cardamom starts to brown. Add the onions and cook over a medium heat for 15 minutes, or until the onions are golden and the oil starts to separate from the onions.

Add the chicken and cook it for 5 minutes, or until it is browned. Add the cashew paste and cook it over a medium heat, stirring constantly, for 5 minutes, or until the oil separates from the sauce.

Add the cream and 250 ml/9 fl oz/1 cup of water, then cover and simmer the pan over a medium heat for 30 minutes, or until the chicken is tender. Serve the dish sprinkled with the fresh coriander leaves.

mustard tomato chicken

cashew chicken

chicken with apricots and cashews

This recipe reminds me more of a casserole than a curry. It is also wonderful made with lamb shanks, but of course you would need to extend the cooking time for an hour or so. Serve the dish with plenty of naan bread.

Preparation time: 20 minutes,
cooking time: 1 hour, serves 4–6

1 kg/2 lb 4 oz mixed chicken pieces
2 red onions, chopped
2 garlic cloves, chopped
3 cm/1¼ inch piece ginger, peeled and chopped
2 tablespoons vegetable oil
1 teaspoon garam masala
2 tomatoes, chopped
375 ml/13 fl oz/generous 1½ cups chicken stock
200 g/7 oz dried apricots
1 tablespoon white vinegar
2 tablespoons grated palm sugar or brown sugar
½ teaspoon salt
150 g/5½ oz/1 cup raw cashews

Score the thickest part of the chicken pieces to ensure it cooks evenly.

Put the onions, garlic and ginger into a food processor and blend them to form a smooth paste. Heat the oil in a pan, add the garlic paste and cook over a medium heat for 5 minutes, or until the oil separates from the paste. Add the garam masala and chicken and cook over a medium heat for 5 minutes, or until the chicken browns.

Add the tomatoes, stock, apricots, vinegar, sugar and salt to the pan and bring it to the boil, then cover and simmer for 20 minutes. Remove the lid and cook for a further 20 minutes, or until the chicken is tender and the sauce has thickened slightly. Stir through half the cashews and sprinkle the rest over the top just before serving.

coriander chicken masala

Ground coriander forms the base for a lot of Indian curries. Here I have used both fresh coriander (cilantro) and dried coriander to flavour the chicken. Yoghurt gives the dish a slightly sour flavour.

Preparation time: 15 minutes, cooking time: 40 minutes, serves 4–6

2 red onions, roughly chopped
80 g/2¾ oz/1⅓ cups fresh coriander (cilantro) leaves and stalks, roughly chopped
2 garlic cloves
2 small green chillies
2 tablespoons vegetable oil
2 teaspoons ground coriander
1 teaspoon ground cumin
½ teaspoon turmeric
pinch saffron threads
500 g/1 lb 2 oz chicken thigh fillets
400 g/14 oz natural (plain) yoghurt
1 teaspoon sugar

Put the onions, coriander, garlic and chillies into a food processor and process to form a smooth paste. You may need to add some water to the mix to form the paste, depending on how much moisture is in the onions.

Heat the oil in a large pan, add the onion and coriander mixture and cook over a medium heat for 10 minutes, or until the oil starts to separate from the onions. Add the spices and cook for 5 minutes, or until fragrant.

Add the chicken to the pan and cook for 5 minutes, or until browned. Then add the yoghurt and sugar and simmer, covered, for 15 minutes, or until the chicken is tender.

spicy chicken noodle soup

Derived from Malaysia, this dish is eaten there morning, noon and night. It is a meal in a bowl that consists usually of noodles topped with a spicy coconut broth teamed with chicken or seafood. Here is my version of this traditional dish.

Preparation time: 10 minutes, cooking time: 30 minutes, serves 4

100 g/3½ oz dried rice vermicelli
1 tablespoon vegetable oil
2 tablespoons laksa paste or red curry paste
500 ml/18 fl oz/generous 2 cups coconut milk
500 ml/18 fl oz/generous 2 cups chicken stock
2 chicken breast fillets, thinly sliced
200 g/7 oz mangetout (snow peas)
100 g/3½ oz oyster mushrooms
150 g/5½ oz bean sprouts
1 tablespoon sambal olek (chilli paste), to serve (optional)
1 cucumber, thinly sliced, to serve
3 tablespoons fried Asian shallots, to serve
1 tablespoon fresh Vietnamese mint leaves, to serve

Put the vermicelli into a large heatproof bowl, cover it with boiling water and allow it to stand for 10 minutes, or until the noodles are soft, then drain well.

Heat the oil in a wok or large pan, add the laksa or curry paste and cook over a medium heat for 3–5 minutes, or until fragrant. Add the coconut milk, stock and chicken, bring the mixture to the boil, then reduce the heat and simmer for 10 minutes. Add the mangetout and mushrooms and simmer for 3 minutes, or until the mangetout are tender.

Divide the noodles and bean sprouts between the bowls, top with the chicken mixture, a spoonful of sambal olek if desired, then the cucumber, Asian shallots and the Vietnamese mint leaves. Serve immediately.

coriander chicken masala

spicy chicken noodle soup

chicken, corn and bamboo shoot curry

chicken, corn and bamboo shoot curry

I discovered this curry on my last trip to Thailand while researching this book and immediately fell in love with it. Yellow curry paste is a mild curry paste available in Asian food stores. If you can't find it, you can use red curry paste instead.

Preparation time: 10 minutes,
cooking time: 30 minutes, serves 4–6

125 ml/4 fl oz/½ cup coconut cream
1 tablespoon yellow curry paste
500 g/1 lb 2 oz chicken thigh fillets, cut into thick slices
500 ml/18 fl oz/generous 2 cups coconut milk
125 g/4½ oz snake beans or green beans, sliced
100 g/3½ oz fresh baby corn, halved
230 g/8¼ oz can bamboo shoots, drained
250 g/9 oz cherry tomatoes
1 tablespoon Thai fish sauce
1½ tablespoons grated palm sugar or brown sugar
20 g/¾ oz/⅓ cup fresh Thai basil leaves or coriander (cilantro) leaves, to serve

Heat the wok, add the coconut cream and curry paste and cook, stirring regularly, over a medium heat for 3–5 minutes, or until the curry paste starts to separate from the coconut cream and becomes fragrant.

Add the chicken and cook for 5 minutes, or until it starts to brown. Next add the coconut milk, beans, corn, bamboo shoots and cherry tomatoes and bring the mixture to the boil, then reduce the heat and simmer for 10 minutes, or until the chicken is tender.

Season the curry with the fish sauce and sugar and simmer for a further 10 minutes. Serve the dish topped with the Thai basil or coriander leaves.

sticky chicken and peanut spicy stir-fry

This is a quick and easy, sweet, stir-fry curry. If broccolini is not available, you can substitute an Asian green such as bok choy, choy sum or pak choi – add them at the end, as they only take a couple of minutes to cook.

Preparation time: 15 minutes,
cooking time: 20 minutes, serves 4

1 tablespoon vegetable oil
1 tablespoon red curry paste
2 garlic cloves, sliced
1 tablespoon grated fresh ginger
3 spring onions (scallions), sliced
500 g/1 lb 2 oz chicken breast fillets, sliced
1 carrot, sliced
1 red pepper (bell pepper), sliced
1 bunch broccolini, roughly chopped
125 ml/4 fl oz/½ cup Thai sweet chilli sauce
2 tablespoons Thai fish sauce
2 tablespoons lime juice
80 g/2¾ oz/generous ½ cup roasted peanuts
2 tablespoons fresh coriander (cilantro) leaves, to serve

Heat the oil in a wok, add the red curry paste, garlic, ginger and spring onions and stir-fry for 3 minutes. Add the chicken and stir-fry for a further 5 minutes, or until browned.

Add the vegetables and 2 tablespoons of water and cook for 5 minutes. Combine the sweet chilli sauce, fish sauce, lime juice and peanuts, then pour the mixture into the wok and bring it to the boil. Remove the wok from the heat, top it with the coriander leaves and serve the dish immediately.

sticky chicken and peanut spicy stir fry

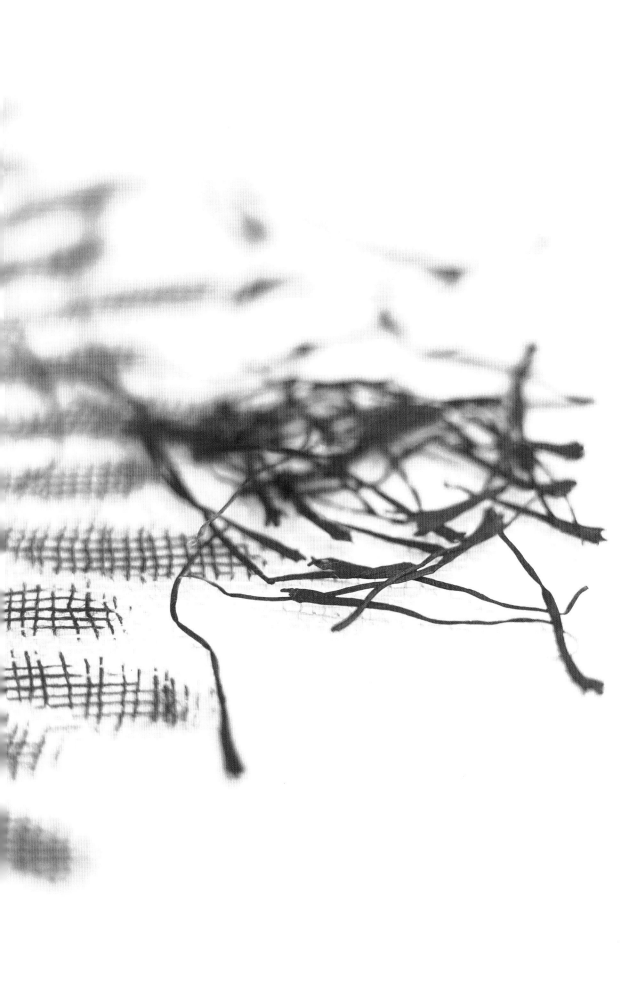

lamb, pork and beef

lamb with cardamom and apricots

Cardamom is a commonly used spice in Indian cooking in both sweet and savoury dishes. Bruise the pods with the side of your cooking knife, as this allows the aroma to be released into the food.

Preparation time: 20 minutes, cooking time: 1 hour, serves 4–6

2 red onions, chopped
2 tablespoons grated fresh ginger
3 garlic cloves
2 tablespoons vegetable oil
1 teaspoon garam masala
6 green cardamom pods, bruised
1 cinnamon stick
750 g/1lb 10 oz cubed leg of lamb
2 tomatoes, chopped
pinch saffron threads
150 g/5½ oz/1 cup dried apricots
1 teaspoon lemon juice

Put the onions, ginger and garlic into a food processor and process until smooth. Heat the oil in a pan, add the onion paste and cook over a medium heat for 15 minutes, or until browned. Add the spices and cook for 5 minutes, or until fragrant.

Add the meat and cook for 5 minutes, or until browned. Stir in the tomatoes, 250 ml/9 fl oz/ generous 1 cup of water, saffron and apricots, cover and simmer for 40 minutes, or until the lamb is tender. Finally, season with lemon juice.

lamb, pork and beef

keema

There are many different versions of this curry, as recipes vary from one region to another due to the availability of fresh produce. Traditionally this recipe is made using lamb, but it can also be made using minced beef.

Preparation time: 20 minutes,
cooking time: 50 minutes, serves 4–6

3 tablespoons vegetable oil
2 onions, finely chopped
1 tablespoon grated fresh ginger
2 garlic cloves, chopped
1–2 small green chillies, seeded and chopped
1 cinnamon stick
3 cloves
750 g/1 lb 10 oz lamb mince
1½ tablespoons ground coriander
1 teaspoon ground cumin
½ teaspoon turmeric
2 medium potatoes, peeled and cubed
200 g/7 oz chopped tomatoes
200 g/7 oz natural (plain) yoghurt
150 g/5½ oz/scant 1½ cups fresh or frozen peas
2 tablespoons chopped fresh coriander
(cilantro)

Heat the oil in a large frying pan, add the onions and cook it over a medium heat for 15 minutes, or until it is browned. Add the ginger, garlic, chillies, cinnamon and cloves and cook these for 3 minutes.

Add the lamb to the pan and cook it over a high heat until it is browned. Stir in the ground coriander, cumin and turmeric and cook for a further 2 minutes, or until fragrant.

Add the potatoes, tomatoes and 250 ml/9 fl oz/ 1 cup of water to the pan, then simmer it, covered, for 20 minutes. Remove the lid, add the yoghurt, peas and coriander and cook for 10 minutes, or until the oil has separated from the sauce.

tandoori lamb cutlets

These cutlets (chops) are always a hit at barbecues, although the marinade can also be used to baste a leg of lamb. I like using a barbecue (grill), as it gives the smoky flavour you would usually get from foods cooked in a tandoor.

Preparation time: 10 minutes + 4 hours marinating, cooking time: 10 minutes, serves 4–6

12 lamb cutlets (chops)
4 tablespoons tandoori paste
1 tablespoon lemon juice
½ teaspoon garam masala
1 teaspoon ground coriander
2 tablespoons grated fresh ginger
4 garlic cloves, chopped
250 g/9 oz/1 cup natural (plain) yoghurt
naan bread, to serve
mango chutney, to serve

Trim the cutlets of any excess fat or sinew. Combine the tandoori paste, lemon juice, garam masala, coriander, ginger, garlic and yoghurt in a mixing bowl. Add the lamb cutlets to the marinade and gently mix to coat them in it. Cover and refrigerate for a minimum of 4 hours – preferably overnight.

Cook the cutlets on a barbecue (grill) or under a preheated grill (broiler) set on a high heat for 5–10 minutes, or until cooked to your liking. Serve with naan bread and mango chutney.

lamb, pork and beef

kaffir lime beef curry

Used extensively throughout Thailand, kaffir lime leaves add a unique aromatic flavour to this dish. If you cannot buy them fresh, use dry, but you may need to increase the quantity slightly.

Preparation time: 15 minutes, cooking time: 15 minutes, serves 4

1 tablespoon vegetable oil
1–2 tablespoons green curry paste
500 g/1 lb 2 oz rump steak, sliced
2 stalks lemongrass, bruised
12 kaffir lime leaves, finely shredded
1 onion, sliced
400 g/14 oz can coconut milk
200 g/7 oz mangetout (snow peas)
250 g/9 oz broccoli florets
1 tablespoon Thai fish sauce
1 tablespoon grated palm sugar or brown sugar

Heat the oil in a wok, add the curry paste and cook it over a medium heat for 3–5 minutes, or until fragrant.

Add the steak to the wok and cook for 3–5 minutes, or until browned. Add the lemongrass, lime leaves and onion and cook for 3 minutes, or until the onion is soft.

Stir in the coconut milk, mangetout and broccoli and simmer for 5 minutes, or until the vegetables are soft. Season the dish with the fish sauce and sugar.

quick masaman beef curry

This is a truly delicious traditional beef curry. The ground peanuts are used to thicken the curry while the tamarind gives the curry a sour taste; if you cannot find it, use lime juice instead.

Preparation time: 15 minutes, cooking time: 25 minutes, serves 4

1 tablespoon vegetable oil
2 tablespoons masaman curry paste (see page 152)
250 g/9 oz rump steak, cubed
2 potatoes, chopped
1 onion, chopped
250 ml/9 fl oz/1 cup coconut cream
1 teaspoon salt
2 tablespoons grated palm sugar or brown sugar
1 tablespoon Thai fish sauce
70 g/2¼ oz/scant ½ cup ground roasted peanuts
250 ml/9 fl oz/1 cup coconut milk
2 tablespoons tamarind concentrate

Heat the oil in a wok, add the curry paste and cook over a low heat for 3 minutes, or until fragrant. Increase the heat slightly and add the beef, potatoes and onion and cook for 5 minutes, or until the beef browns.

Stir in the coconut cream, salt, sugar, fish sauce, peanuts, coconut milk, and 125 ml/4 fl oz/½ cup of water. Bring the mixture to the boil, reduce the heat and simmer for 10 minutes, or until the potatoes are cooked. Add the tamarind and cook for a further 5 minutes before serving.

kaffir lime beef curry

quick masaman beef curry

goan pork vindaloo

This recipe is a favourite of residents in the Goa region. Vindaloo means vinegar and garlic and it is a very spicy dish, so be warned. You can use a store-bought vindaloo paste if you like – simply use 2 tablespoons with the vinegar.

Preparation time: 25 minutes + 1 hour marinating, cooking time: 50 minutes, serves 4–6

750 g/1lb 10 oz pork fillet, cubed
1½ tablespoons ground coriander
1 teaspoon ground cumin
½ teaspoon hot chilli powder
½ teaspoon black pepper
¼ teaspoon turmeric
80 ml/2¾ fl oz/scant ⅓ cup coconut vinegar
or white vinegar
1 tablespoon balsamic vinegar
3 tablespoons vegetable oil
2 red onions, thinly sliced
1 tablespoon grated fresh ginger
12 garlic cloves, chopped
3 ripe, medium-sized tomatoes, chopped
2–3 small green chillies, seeded and sliced
1 teaspoon grated palm sugar or brown sugar

Put the pork, spices and vinegars into a bowl and allow to marinate for 1 hour.

Heat the oil in a large pan, add the onions and cook over a medium heat for 15 minutes, or until browned. Add the ginger and garlic and cook for 2 minutes.

Add the marinated pork, tomatoes, chillies, sugar and 250 ml/9 fl oz/1 cup of water to the pan, then cover it and simmer for 30 minutes or until the meat is tender.

pork satay

All over Thailand there are stalls selling satay, pork, chicken, beef, tofu, octopus and salt squid. This is a mild satay – you can add another spoon of red curry paste if you prefer hotter dishes.

Preparation time: 20 minutes + 30 minutes soaking, cooking time: 20 minutes, serves 4

500 g/1 lb 2 oz pork fillet
1 tablespoon vegetable oil
1–2 tablespoons red curry paste
70 g/2¼ oz/scant ½ cup coarsely ground roasted peanuts
1 tablespoon peanut butter
400 ml/14 fl oz/1¾ cups coconut milk
1 tablespoon Thai fish sauce
2 teaspoons lime juice
1 tablespoon grated palm sugar or brown sugar

Soak 12 bamboo skewers in cold water for 30 minutes to stop them burning when they are placed on the barbecue (grill). Cut the pork into thin strips and thread onto the soaked bamboo skewers.

Heat the oil in a wok, add the curry paste and cook over a medium heat for 3–5 minutes, or until fragrant. Add the peanuts, peanut butter, coconut milk, fish sauce, lime juice and sugar. Simmer the mixture for 10 minutes, or until it has thickened slightly.

Cook the skewered pork on a lightly oiled barbecue (grill) for 2–3 minutes on each side, or until tender. Serve the pork with pots of the peanut curry dipping sauce.

simple indian curry

This recipe is very straightforward – you simply fry a few spices then leave the dish to simmer. Make sure you use a cut of meat that is not too lean, as it will toughen with extended cooking.

Preparation time: 10 minutes,
cooking time: 1 hour, serves 4–6

2 tablespoons vegetable oil
1 onion, chopped
1 teaspoon ground coriander
2 teaspoons ground cumin
1 teaspoon turmeric
1 teaspoon garam masala
1 teaspoon crushed garlic
500 g/1 lb 2 oz topside steak, cut into cubes
400 g/14 oz can chopped tomatoes
150 g/5½ oz green beans, cut into
4 cm/1½ inch lengths
1 medium-sized courgette (zucchini), sliced
150 g/5½ oz sweet potato, diced

Heat the oil in a pan, add the chopped onion, spices and garlic and fry for 2–3 minutes. Add the beef and cook for 5 minutes, or until brown. Add the canned tomatoes and 250 ml/9 fl oz/1 cup of water and simmer for 45 minutes. Finally, add the vegetables, and simmer for 10–15 minutes, or until the meat and vegetables are tender.

madras lamb curry

There are a variety of good-quality prepared Madras curry pastes available in supermarkets, which help to make this a quick and easy curry to prepare. The lamb shoulder can be replaced with lamb leg if you want to use a leaner cut.

Preparation time: 20 minutes, cooking time: 1 hour 20 minutes, serves 4–6

2 tablespoons vegetable oil
1 red onion, chopped
1 tablespoon grated fresh ginger
2 garlic cloves, chopped
2 tablespoons Madras curry paste
1 kg/2 lb 4 oz chopped lamb shoulder
400 g/14 oz can chopped tomatoes
400 ml/14 fl oz/1¾ cups coconut milk
1 cinnamon stick
6 cloves

Heat the oil in a large pan, add the onion and cook over a medium heat for 10 minutes, or until browned. Add the ginger, garlic and curry paste and cook for 3 minutes, or until the paste is fragrant.

Add the lamb to the pan and cook it over a medium heat for 5 minutes, or until it is browned. Stir in the tomatoes, coconut milk, cinnamon and cloves, then cover and simmer for 1 hour or until the meat is tender.

beef rendang

This is an exquisite beef curry – a few years back I was travelling in Indonesia and came upon a wonderful cooking school that shared this recipe with me. It does have a bite to it, so you may want to reduce the amount of chillies.

Preparation time: 20 minutes + 15 minutes soaking + 30 minutes marinating, cooking time: 1–1½ hours, serves 6–8

30 g/1 oz/½ cup large dried red chillies
1 teaspoon coriander seeds
1 tablespoon chopped fresh ginger
2 teaspoons ground cumin
½ teaspoon ground cloves
¼ teaspoon turmeric
3 garlic cloves, peeled
10 red Asian shallots, roughly chopped
1 kg/2 lb 4 oz topside steak, cubed
30 g/1 oz/⅓ cup desiccated (dry unsweetened) coconut
500 ml/18 fl oz/generous 2 cups coconut milk
2 stalks lemongrass, chopped
1 tablespoon chopped galangal (optional)
1 teaspoon salt
2 teaspoons grated palm sugar or brown sugar

Soak the chillies in boiling water for 15 minutes, or until soft, then drain well. Roughly chop them and put them into a food processor. Add the coriander seeds, ginger, cumin, cloves, turmeric, garlic and shallots and process to form a smooth paste. You may need to add a little water to bring the paste together.

Put the meat into a bowl, add the spice paste and mix to combine. Cover and allow the meat to marinate for 30 minutes.

Place the meat, coconut, coconut milk, lemongrass, galangal (if using), salt and sugar into a wok and bring the mixture to the boil, reduce the heat and simmer, uncovered, until most of the gravy has evaporated and the oil has separated from the sauce. Continue to cook, stirring regularly, until the curry becomes quite dry.

madras lamb curry

beef rendang

chilli pork with basil

lamb saag

chilli pork with basil

This is a curry from my favourite curry shop in Bangkok, and one that regularly appears at most curry stands. You could use chicken mince to replace the pork if you like.

Preparation time: 10 minutes, cooking time: 25 minutes, serves 4

1 tablespoon vegetable oil
500 g/1 lb 2 oz pork mince
3 garlic cloves, chopped
1 tablespoon red curry paste
500 ml/18 fl oz/generous 2 cups coconut milk
100 g/3½ oz snake beans or green beans, sliced
2 tablespoons Thai fish sauce
2 tablespoons grated palm sugar or brown sugar
10 g/¼ oz/scant ¼ cup fresh Thai basil leaves or regular basil
sliced red chilli, to serve

Heat the oil in a wok over a medium-high heat, add the mince and fry for 5 minutes, or until it is browned. Add the garlic and curry paste and cook for 3 minutes, or until the curry paste is fragrant.

Stir in the coconut milk, snake beans, fish sauce and sugar. Bring the mixture to the boil, reduce the heat and simmer, uncovered, for 15 minutes, or until the oil separates from the sauce. Add the basil leaves, then garnish with the sliced red chilli to serve.

lamb saag

In India this dish is made using amaranth, which is a leafy green very similar to spinach. The best result comes from using fresh spinach, but you can use frozen spinach as an alternative.

Preparation time: 20 minutes + 30 minutes marinating, cooking time: 1 hour 15 minutes, serves 4–6

500 g/1 lb 2 oz cubed leg of lamb
55 g/2 oz/¼ cup natural (plain) yoghurt
1 tablespoon ground coriander
1 teaspoon ground cumin
½ teaspoon ground cayenne
½ teaspoon ground black pepper
¼ teaspoon turmeric
2 tablespoons vegetable oil
1 red onion, finely chopped
1 cinnamon stick
3 cloves
2 teaspoons grated fresh ginger
2 garlic cloves, crushed
500 g/1 lb 2 oz English spinach, roughly chopped

Put the lamb, yoghurt and spices into a bowl and mix to combine. Cover and allow the meat to marinate for 30 minutes.

Heat the oil in a large pan, add the onion and cook over a medium heat for 15 minutes, or until browned. Add the meat and cook it for 5 minutes, or until it changes colour.

Add the cinnamon, cloves, ginger, garlic, spinach and 250 ml/9 fl oz/1 cup of water and simmer, covered, for 45 minutes. Remove the lid and cook for a further 10 minutes or until the sauce thickens.

* Note: you could add 400 g/14 oz of canned tomatoes instead of the water for a richer-flavoured curry.

lamb, pork and beef

rogan josh

The direct translation of this dish is fat (rogan) heat (josh). It uses asafoetida, which is a strong-smelling powder with a mild, garlic-like flavour. As well as adding flavour, Indians use it for its digestive properties.

Preparation time: 20 minutes + 4 hours marinating, cooking time: 55 minutes, serves 4–6

1 kg/2 lb 4 oz lamb shoulder, cubed
2 tablespoons ginger garlic paste (see page 152)
250 g/9 oz/1 cup natural (plain) yoghurt
1 teaspoon hot chilli powder
¼ teaspoon asafoetida (optional)
2 teaspoons ground cumin
2 teaspoons ground coriander
2 tablespoons ghee or butter
1 red onion, chopped
1 teaspoon cardamom pods, bruised
2 bay leaves
4 cloves
1 cinnamon stick
1 teaspoon salt
¼ teaspoon saffron threads
2 tablespoons chopped fresh coriander (cilantro)
½ teaspoon garam masala

Put the lamb, ginger garlic paste, yoghurt, chilli, asafoetida (if using), cumin and coriander into a bowl, then cover and allow to marinate for a minimum of 4 hours – preferably overnight.

Heat the ghee in a pan, add the onion and cook over a medium heat for 10 minutes, or until golden. Add the marinated lamb, spices and 125 ml/4 fl oz/½ cup of water, cover the pan and simmer for 45 minutes, or until the meat is tender.

Stir through the coriander and sprinkle the dish with the garam masala. Cover the dish and allow it to stand for 5 minutes before serving.

penang beef

One of the more popular curry dishes in Thailand, which some believe is of Malay origin. This mild curry is most commonly made using beef, though it is also delicious cooked with chicken or pork.

Preparation time: 30 minutes + 15 minutes soaking, cooking time: 20 minutes, serves 4–6

3 tablespoons peanuts
5 large dried red chillies
1 teaspoon sea salt
1 tablespoon chopped galangal (optional)
1 teaspoon chopped coriander root
1 tablespoon chopped lemongrass
2 tablespoons chopped Asian shallots
2 tablespoons chopped garlic
2 tablespoons vegetable oil
500 g/1 lb 2 oz rump steak, cut into thin strips
500 ml/18 fl oz/2 cups coconut milk
1 tablespoon grated palm sugar or brown sugar
1 tablespoon Thai fish sauce

Roast the peanuts until golden. Allow them to cool thoroughly, then grind them in a mortar and pestle or food processor.

Split the chillies down their centres and remove the seeds and white membranes (this is best done while wearing plastic gloves). Soak the chillies in cold water for 15 minutes, then drain and pat dry.

Put the chillies, salt, galangal (if using), coriander, lemongrass, shallots and garlic into a food processor and process to form a smooth paste.

Heat the oil in a wok, add the paste and cook it over a medium heat for 5 minutes, then add the beef and fry for 5 minutes, or until browned. Add the coconut milk, sugar and fish sauce and cook until the oil floats to the surface of the coconut milk.

rogan josh

penang beef

lamb korma

This is a wonderful mild curry that all the family will enjoy. The cashews give the dish a creamy texture – if you want a stronger cashew flavour, roast them before processing (allow them to cool). You could also use blanched almonds instead.

Preparation time: 20 minutes + 30 minutes marinating, cooking time: 1 hour, serves 4–6

1 kg/2 lb 4oz cubed leg of lamb
55 g/2 oz/¼ cup natural (plain) yoghurt
1 tablespoon ground coriander
1 teaspoon ground cumin
½ teaspoon ground cardamom
2 teaspoons grated fresh ginger
2 cloves garlic, chopped
80 g/2¾ oz/½ cup cashews
3 tablespoons vegetable oil
2 onions, thinly sliced
1 cinnamon stick
½ teaspoon salt
400 ml/14 fl oz/1¾ cups coconut cream

Put the lamb, yoghurt and spices into a bowl and mix to combine. Cover and allow the meat to marinate for 30 minutes.

Put the ginger, garlic and cashews into a spice grinder or food processor and process until smooth – you may need to add a couple of tablespoons of water in order to bring the mixture together.

Heat the oil in a pan, add the onions and cook over a medium heat for 5 minutes, or until browned. Add the marinated meat and cook for 5 minutes, or until the meat begins to brown. Next, add the cashew paste, cinnamon, salt, coconut cream and 125 ml/4 fl oz/½ cup of water to the pan and simmer, covered, for 30 minutes. Remove the lid and cook for a further 20 minutes, or until the sauce is thick.

lamb biryani

Most of the travelling I did while researching this book in India was by train. Biryani was regularly served for dinner on the trains, and it was so delicious it inspired me to create my own biryani for lamb.

Preparation time: 15 minutes, cooking time: 50 minutes, serves 4–6

2 tablespoons vegetable oil
1 onion, chopped
1 tablespoon grated fresh ginger
2 garlic cloves, crushed
1 tablespoon ground coriander
1 teaspoon ground cumin
1 teaspoon ground cinnamon
1 teaspoon turmeric
500 g/1 lb 2 oz lean lamb, cubed
300 g/10½ oz/1½ cups basmati rice
½ teaspoon saffron threads
1 litre/32 fl oz/4 cups chicken stock
150 g/5½ oz/1½ cups frozen peas
200 g/7 oz cauliflower florets
55 g/2 oz/scant ½ cup raisins
65 g/2¼ oz/scant ½ cup pistachios, roughly chopped

Preheat your oven to 180°C/350°F/gas mark 4. Heat the oil in large non-stick ovenproof pan and cook the onion over a medium heat for 10 minutes, or until it is golden brown. Add the ginger and garlic and cook for 2 minutes, or until soft.

Add the coriander, cumin, cinnamon and turmeric to the pan and cook for 1 minute. Add the lamb and cook for 5 minutes, or until browned. Stir in the rice and saffron, cook for 1 minute, then add the stock, peas, cauliflower and raisins and bring to a simmer.

Cover the pan and place it in the oven for 25–30 minutes, or until the stock is absorbed and the rice is cooked. Remove it from the oven and let it stand for 5 minutes. Fold through the chopped pistachios just before serving the dish.

chiang mai pork curry

Chiang Mai is a town in north Thailand and this is a traditional dish from there. I like it because it uses water instead of coconut milk, which is unusual. The tamarind also gives it a slightly sour finish. Yes, it is as easy as it looks.

Preparation time: 20 minutes + 30 minutes marinating, cooking time: 30 minutes, serves 4–6

500 g/1 lb 2 oz pork fillet, cubed
2 tablespoons Thai fish sauce
2 tablespoons grated palm sugar or brown sugar
3 tablespoons red curry paste
2 tablespoons vegetable oil
85 g/3 oz/generous ½ cup roasted peanuts
30 g/1 oz piece ginger, peeled and julienned
2 tablespoons tamarind concentrate

Put the pork, fish sauce, sugar and curry paste into a bowl, cover and allow the pork to marinate for 30 minutes.

Heat the oil in a wok, add the marinated pork and stir-fry for 5 minutes, or until the pork changes colour. Add 500 ml/18 fl oz/ generous 2 cups of water, the peanuts, ginger and tamarind and bring to the boil, then reduce the heat and simmer for 20 minutes, or until the pork is tender and the sauce has reduced slightly.

pork, tomato and potato red curry

I discovered this curry on my latest trip to Thailand, again in my favourite curry shop in Bangkok. There is always something different each time I visit. I have only one problem – I want to try every dish but can only eat so many meals a day!

Preparation time: 10 minutes,
cooking time: 30 minutes, serves 4–6

2 tablespoons vegetable oil
2 tablespoons red curry paste
500 g/1lb 2 oz pork fillet, cubed
1 onion, sliced
400 ml/14 fl oz/1¾ cups coconut milk
2 potatoes, cut into 3 cm/1¼ inch pieces
200 g/7 oz cherry tomatoes
1 tablespoon Thai fish sauce
2 tablespoons grated palm sugar or brown sugar

Heat the oil in a wok, add the curry paste and cook it over a medium heat for 3 minutes, or until the oil separates from the paste.

Add the pork and onion to the wok and cook for 5 minutes, or until the pork begins to brown and the onion is softened.

Next add the coconut milk, potatoes, tomatoes, fish sauce and sugar in the wok. Bring it to the boil, reduce the heat and simmer, uncovered, for 20 minutes, or until the pork is soft and the oil separates from the coconut milk.

fragrant beef and pumpkin curry

Although this is a Thai-style curry, the flavour base comes from India. If you use masaman paste, it will have a nuttier flavour than if you use red curry paste. The tamarind is not essential but adds a nice sour finish that contrasts well with the pumpkin.

Preparation time: 20 minutes,
cooking time: 25 minutes, serves 4–6

1 tablespoon vegetable oil
4 tablespoons masaman curry paste
(see page 152) or red curry paste
500 g/1 lb 2 oz rump steak, cubed
1 onion, cut into wedges
2 cinnamon sticks
500 ml/18 fl oz/generous 2 cups coconut milk
450 g/1 lb chopped pumpkin
200 g/7 oz fresh or canned baby corn spears, halved
1 tablespoon tamarind concentrate (optional)
2 tablespoons Thai fish sauce
2 tablespoons grated palm sugar or brown sugar
fresh coriander (cilantro) leaves, to serve

Heat the oil in a wok, add the curry paste and cook it over a medium heat for 3–5 minutes, or until fragrant.

Add the beef to the wok and stir-fry it for 5 minutes, or until it is browned. Add the onion and cinnamon and cook for 3 minutes, or until the onion is soft.

Next add the coconut milk, pumpkin, corn, tamarind (if using), fish sauce and sugar and simmer for 15 minutes, or until the pumpkin is tender. Serve the dish topped with the coriander leaves.

pork, tomato and potato red curry

fragrant beef and pumpkin curry

red pork and pineapple curry

This is a quick stir-fry version of basic red beef curry. Red curry is usually milder than green, and the spiciness of this recipe is tempered with the addition of fresh pineapple.

Preparation time: 15 minutes, cooking time: 20 minutes, serves 4

1 tablespoon groundnut (peanut) oil
2 tablespoons red curry paste
500 g/1lb 2 oz lean pork fillets, cubed
400 ml/14 fl oz/1¾ cups coconut milk
200 g/7 oz mangetout (snow peas)
1 red pepper (bell pepper), sliced
320 g/11 oz chopped fresh pineapple
2 tablespoons Thai fish sauce
1 tablespoon lime juice
2 tablespoons grated palm sugar or brown sugar
10 g/¼ oz/scant ¼ cup fresh Thai basil leaves
or coriander (cilantro), to serve

Heat the oil in a wok, add the curry paste and cook it over a medium heat until fragrant. Add the pork and cook it for 3–5 minutes, or until it begins to brown. Stir in the coconut milk, vegetables and pineapple, bring to the boil, then reduce the heat and simmer for 10 minutes.

Season the dish with the fish sauce, lime juice and sugar. Serve it topped with the Thai basil leaves or you can use coriander, which works well with the pineapple.

fish and seafood

lemongrass chilli mussels

It is really important when cooking mussels that you scrub them properly – this is best done with a wire scourer. Make sure you discard any mussels that do not open after cooking, as they may not be suitable to eat.

Preparation time: 15 minutes,
cooking time: 20 minutes, serves 4–6

1 kg/2 lb 4 oz mussels
1 tablespoon vegetable oil
2 garlic cloves, sliced
2 stalks lemongrass, finely chopped
(use the white part only)
2 large red chillies, seeded and thinly sliced
2 teaspoons green curry paste
4 spring onions (scallions), cut into
3 cm/1¼ inch pieces
500 ml/18 fl oz/generous 2 cups fish stock
1 tablespoon Thai fish sauce
2 teaspoons grated palm sugar or brown sugar
2 tablespoons lime juice

Scrub and remove the beards from the mussels. Heat the oil in a wok, add the garlic, lemongrass, chillies and curry paste and stir-fry over a medium heat for 3 minutes, or until the curry paste is fragrant. Add the spring onions and cook for 2 minutes, or until they are soft.

Add the mussels, stock, fish sauce, sugar and lime juice to the wok, cover and simmer for 10 minutes, or until the mussels open.

fish and seafood

fish mollee

The tamarind gives this true southern curry a wonderful sour finish that cuts through the richness of the coconut milk. Make sure you use a nice firm fish that will hold together during the cooking process.

Preparation time: 15 minutes,
cooking time: 25–30 minutes, serves 4–6

2 tablespoons vegetable oil
½ teaspoon fenugreek seeds
10 curry leaves
2 small green chillies, split lengthwise
1 red onion, sliced
1 tablespoon tamarind concentrate
½ teaspoon turmeric
½ teaspoon salt
½ teaspoon cracked black pepper
¼ teaspoon hot chilli powder
375 ml/13 fl oz/1½ cups coconut milk
500 g/1 lb 2 oz boneless firm white fish fillets (such as snapper or cod), cut into large pieces
1 medium-sized ripe tomato, chopped

Heat the oil in a pan, add the fenugreek seeds and cook them over a medium heat until they begin to pop. Add the curry leaves, green chillies and onion and cook for 10 minutes, or until the onion is golden.

Add the tamarind, turmeric, salt, pepper, chilli powder and half the coconut milk to the pan. Bring it to the boil, reduce the heat, add the fish and cook for 5–10 minutes, turning the fish a couple of times during cooking.

Place the tomatoes in the pan, cover and cook for 5 minutes. Add the remaining coconut milk and simmer, uncovered, for 10 minutes, or until the oil separates from the curry.

red curry fish cakes

I have vivid memories of my sister Paulie and I walking through the weekend market in Bangkok with a plastic bag full of miniature fish cakes. I have been trying for years to perfect these tasty morsels, and this recipe comes pretty close.

Preparation time: 20 minutes,
cooking time: 15 minutes, serves 4–6

500 g/1 lb 2 oz boneless red snapper fillets or orange roughy
4 tablespoons red curry paste
1 egg, lightly beaten
3 tablespoons sliced snake beans or green beans
4 kaffir lime leaves, very finely shredded
1 tablespoon Thai fish sauce
2 teaspoons caster (superfine) sugar
groundnut (peanut) oil, for deep frying

Put the fish, curry paste and egg into a food processor and process to form a smooth paste. Transfer the paste to a bowl, add the snake beans and lime leaves, then season with the fish sauce and sugar.

Shape tablespoons of the mixture into small balls and flatten them with the palm of your hand. Heat the oil in a wok over a medium heat and deep-fry the fish cakes (in batches) for 3 minutes, or until they are golden brown and cooked right through.

fish mollee

red curry fish cakes

goan prawn (shrimp) curry

Probably the most popular curry on the coast of Goa, this recipe can be cooked with prawns (shrimp) or a firm fleshed fish. It is important that you cook the onions until they caramelize, as this adds sweetness to the dish.

Preparation time: 20 minutes, cooking time: 25 minutes, serves 4–6

30 g/1 oz/½ cup large dried red chillies, seeded
3 teaspoons coriander seeds
1 teaspoon cumin seeds
2 small red onions, chopped
3 garlic cloves
1 tablespoon grated fresh ginger
1 teaspoon turmeric
3 tablespoons vegetable oil
2 small green chillies, split in half
1 kg/2 lb 4 oz medium king prawns (jumbo shrimp), peeled and deveined
2 ripe tomatoes, chopped
500 ml/18 fl oz/generous 2 cups coconut milk
1 teaspoon lemon juice
½ teaspoon salt
½ tablespoon grated palm sugar or brown sugar

Cook the red chillies and coriander and cumin seeds in a dry frying pan set over a medium heat for 3 minutes, or until fragrant. Remove and allow to cool slightly. Transfer them to a food processor or spice grinder, add the onions, garlic, ginger and turmeric and process until smooth – you may need to add a little water to form a thin paste.

Heat the oil in a pan, add the spice paste and cook it over a medium heat for 10 minutes, or until the oil separates from the paste.

Add the chillies, prawns, tomatoes and coconut milk to the pan and simmer, uncovered, for 10 minutes, or until the oil separates from the curry. Season the dish with the lemon juice, salt and sugar before serving.

baked fish in banana leaves

The fish can either be wrapped in banana leaves or simply baked in the oven or on a covered barbecue (grill). Although not what you may traditionally think of as a curry, this recipe uses curry spices to create one of my favourite fish dishes.

Preparation time: 30 minutes,
cooking time: 45 minutes, serves 6

½ teaspoon turmeric
1 teaspoon cracked black pepper
1 teaspoon salt
1 kg/2 lb 4 oz thick firm white boneless fish fillets (such as cod or halibut), cut into 10 cm/4 inch wide pieces
vegetable oil, for shallow frying
5 small green chillies
20 red Asian shallots
4 garlic cloves
3 cm/1¼ inch piece ginger, peeled and chopped
1 red onion, sliced
1 teaspoon ground coriander
½ teaspoon turmeric
1 teaspoon lemon juice
1 tablespoon grated palm sugar or brown sugar
young banana leaves or foil

Preheat the oven to 220°C/425°F/gas mark 7. Combine the turmeric, pepper and salt and rub the mix into both sides of the fish pieces. Heat the oil in a wok and shallow-fry the fish for 2 minutes on each side, or until golden brown. Remove and drain on absorbent kitchen paper. Remove all but 3 tablespoons of the oil.

Put the chillies, shallots, garlic and ginger into a food processor and process to form a smooth paste – you may need a little water to help the paste come together. Heat the remaining oil, add the red onion and cook it for 15 minutes, or until it is caramelized. Add the chilli paste and cook it over a medium heat for 5 minutes. Add the coriander and turmeric and cook until the oil separates from the sauce. Remove the wok from the heat, season the dish with lemon juice and sugar and allow it to cool slightly.

Heat the banana leaves over an open gas flame or under the grill (broiler) until soft and pliable. Spread the paste over both sides of the fish, then wrap it in the banana leaves or foil and secure with string. Put the parcels onto a non-stick baking tray and bake for 10–15 minutes, or until tender.

simple seafood curry

This quick and easy curry can be made using any seafood. The yoghurt is simmered with the tomatoes so will split, but this does not affect the overall taste of the dish (do try to use a thinner yoghurt rather than a thick Greek-style one).

Preparation time: 15 minutes,
cooking time: 25 minutes, serves 4–6

2 tablespoons vegetable oil
1 teaspoon black mustard seeds
1 red onion, chopped
1 teaspoon garam masala
1 teaspoon ground cumin
1 teaspoon ground coriander
½ teaspoon turmeric
½ teaspoon hot chilli powder
750 g/1 lb 10 oz mixed seafood (prawns/shrimp, fish, scallops, squid)
400 g/14 oz can chopped tomatoes
½ teaspoon salt
125 g/4 oz/½ cup natural (plain) yoghurt
1 teaspoon grated palm sugar or brown sugar

Heat the oil in a pan, add the mustard seeds and cook them over a medium heat for 3 minutes, or until they begin to pop. Add the onion and cook it over a medium heat for 5 minutes, or until golden. Next add the garam masala, cumin, coriander, turmeric and chilli powder, then cook for 2 minutes, or until the oil separates from the sauce.

Add the seafood to the pan and cook it until it changes colour (stops being translucent). Add the tomatoes, salt and yoghurt and then simmer, covered, for 10 minutes, or until the seafood is tender. Finally, add the sugar and cook for 2 minutes.

baked fish in banana leaves

simple seafood curry

hot and sour prawn (shrimp) soup

hot and sour prawn (shrimp) soup

This soup is traditionally called Tom Yum Goong. Do not overcook the prawn (shrimp) shells in the stock, or the liquid will turn bitter. You can make the stock in advance and add the prawns (shrimp) just before serving so they remain nice and juicy.

Preparation time: 10 minutes,
cooking time: 20 minutes, serves 4

500 g/1 lb 2 oz medium green prawns (shrimp)
1.25 litres/40 fl oz/5 cups chicken stock
3 stalks lemongrass, bruised
4 kaffir limes leaves, torn
1 tablespoon red curry paste
2 ripe tomatoes, roughly chopped
1 tablespoon Thai fish sauce
3 tablespoons lime juice
2 tablespoons fresh coriander (cilantro) leaves, to serve (optional)

Peel and devein the prawns, leaving the tails intact and reserving the shells.

Put the prawn shells and chicken stock into a pan and bring it to the boil, then reduce the heat and simmer for 10 minutes. Strain and reserve the stock, discarding the shells.

Return the stock to the pan, add the lemongrass, lime leaves, curry paste and prawns, then simmer for 3–5 minutes, or until the prawns are tender. Add the tomatoes and season with the fish sauce and lime juice. Serve topped with coriander leaves (if using).

kerala fish curry

In this recipe, the combination of the sweetness of the shallots and the sharpness of the tamarind works perfectly with the fish. The tomatoes make a welcome relief to coconut-based curries, which seem to dominate in this part of the country.

Preparation time: 15 minutes,
cooking time: 30 minutes, serves 4–6

10 red Asian shallots, chopped
4 garlic cloves
2 cm/¾ inch piece ginger, peeled
3 tablespoons vegetable oil
2 dried red chillies
10 curry leaves
1 teaspoon garam masala
750 g/1 lb 10 oz boneless firm white fish fillets, cut into large pieces
2 ripe tomatoes, chopped
125 ml/4 fl oz/½ cup coconut milk
½ teaspoon salt
1 tablespoon tamarind concentrate
½ tablespoon grated palm sugar or brown sugar
1 or 2 small red chillies, halved, to serve

Put the shallots, garlic and ginger into a food processor and process until smooth – you may need to add a little water to bring it together.

Heat the oil in a pan, add the paste and cook it over a medium heat for 10 minutes, or until the oil separates from the paste.

Add the chillies, curry leaves and garam masala to the pan and cook for 3 minutes. Next add the fish, tomatoes, coconut milk and salt and simmer, covered, for 10 minutes.

Add the tamarind and sugar and simmer uncovered for 5 minutes, or until the oil separates from the sauce. Finally, garnish the dish with the small red chillies.

kerala fish curry

fish and seafood

mussel and squid fry

Each day I was staying in Kochi, Kerala, I would buy squid, mussels, prawns (shrimp) or crab and the fishmonger (fish dealer) would make this for me. I had never tasted anything like it, so was very happy when Reena, my cooking instructor there, taught me to make it.

Preparation time: 20 minutes,
cooking time: 30 minutes, serves 4–6

400 g/14 oz small squid
200 g/7 oz mussel meat
1 teaspoon hot chilli powder
½ teaspoon turmeric
½ teaspoon salt
1 tablespoon ginger garlic paste (see page 152)
2 tablespoons vegetable oil
10 curry leaves
1 teaspoon grated palm sugar or brown sugar

Clean the squid and cut the tubes into rings. Put the squid rings, tentacles, mussels, chilli powder, turmeric, salt and ginger garlic paste into a bowl and mix to combine.

Put the seafood mixture into a wok, cover and cook for 15 minutes, or until it is all tender. Remove the lid and cook, uncovered, over a high heat for a further 10 minutes, or until all the liquid has evaporated.

Add the oil, curry leaves and sugar to the wok, then stir-fry the seafood for 5 minutes, or until the spices are slightly crisp on the outside.

chu chi scallop and fish curry

The shrimp paste smells awful but adds an amazing depth of flavour to the curry. To roast it, wrap it in foil and grill (broil) it for 5 minutes.

Preparation time: 15 minutes,
cooking time: 30 minutes, serves 4–6

500 ml/18 fl oz/generous 2 cups coconut milk (including the cream)
1–2 tablespoons red curry paste
1 teaspoon shrimp paste, roasted (optional)
2 tablespoons Thai fish sauce
1–2 tablespoons grated palm sugar or brown sugar
4 kaffir lime leaves, finely shredded
300 g/10½ oz boneless firm white fish fillets (such as snapper, cod and halibut), cubed
12 scallops with roe removed

Heat a wok, then add the thick coconut cream from the top of a can of coconut milk, as well as the curry paste. Cook them over a medium heat for 5 minutes, or until the coconut cream cracks and the oil floats to the surface.

Add the coconut milk and season the dish with the shrimp paste, fish sauce, sugar and lime leaves, then simmer for 20 minutes, or until the curry has reduced and thickened. Finally, add the fish and scallops and cook for 5 minutes, or until tender.

mussel and squid fry

chu chi scallop and fish curry

deep fried fish with sweet red curry sauce

It is important when deep-frying the fish that you make sure it is absolutely dry first. Use absorbent kitchen paper to do this and pat it thoroughly inside and out. Also make sure you only half-fill the wok with oil: it will rise when you add in the fish.

Preparation time: 15 minutes,
cooking time: 20–25 minutes, serves 4

750 g/1 lb 10 oz whole snapper
groundnut (peanut) oil, for deep frying
2 tablespoons groundnut (peanut) oil
1 onion, chopped
4 garlic cloves, chopped
2 tablespoons red curry paste
1 tablespoon soy sauce
115 g/4 oz/generous ½ cup grated palm sugar or brown sugar
3 tablespoons lime juice
1 large red chilli, thinly sliced, to serve
10 fresh Thai basil leaves or 10 sprigs of coriander (cilantro), to serve

Cut 3 deep incisions on both sides of the fish. Pat it dry with absorbent kitchen paper.

Heat enough groundnut (peanut) oil to deep-fry the fish in a wok over a medium heat until it bubbles around a wooden chopstick when stood upright in the oil. Deep-fry the fish for 3–5 minutes on each side, or until golden and tender. Remove and drain it on absorbent kitchen paper.

To make the sauce, heat the 2 tablespoons of groundnut (peanut) oil in a wok, add the onion, garlic and curry paste and cook over a low heat for 3 minutes, or until fragrant. Add the soy sauce, sugar and lime juice and simmer for 10 minutes, or until the mixture is syrupy.

Pour the curry over the fish and garnish it with the sliced chilli and basil leaves before serving.

vegetables

egg masala

I think every day I was in Kochi in Kerala I ate egg masala and appam (a rice flour pancake) for breakfast, washed down with a cup of chai. Serve this recipe with lots of Indian bread to mop up the delicious juices.

Preparation time: 15 minutes, cooking time: 40 minutes, serves 4–6

3 tablespoons vegetable oil
1 red onion, finely chopped
1 tablespoon ground coriander
½ teaspoon fennel seeds
1 teaspoon garam masala
½ teaspoon hot chilli powder
½ teaspoon turmeric
1 tomato, chopped
½ teaspoon salt
250 ml/9 fl oz/1 cup coconut milk
1 tablespoon tamarind concentrate
8 hard-boiled eggs, peeled

Heat the oil in a pan, add the onion and cook over a medium heat for 10 minutes, or until it is golden. Add the coriander and fennel seeds and cook for 3 minutes, or until fragrant.

Add the garam masala, chilli powder and turmeric and cook for 5 minutes, or until the oil separates from the spices.

Stir in the tomato, salt, 125 ml/4 fl oz/½ cup water, coconut milk and tamarind and simmer, uncovered, for 20 minutes, or until the oil comes away from the sauce. Add the eggs and simmer until they have heated through.

dhal makhan

I am unsure of exactly how many recipes there are for dhal in India; one thing I do know is that you haven't had a full meal until you have eaten dhal. It is a staple of the Indian cuisine. This one is a little decadent so team it with a lighter curry.

Preparation time: 10 minutes,
cooking time: 1 hour, serves 4–6

200 g/7 oz/1 cup moong dhal or yellow split peas (see page 144 for more information)
2 tablespoons ghee or vegetable oil
2 tablespoons ginger garlic paste (see page 152)
400 g/14 oz can tomato purée
2 teaspoon ground coriander
½ teaspoon garam masala
¼ teaspoon grated nutmeg
½ teaspoon salt
125 ml/4 fl oz/½ cup single (light) cream

Cook the moong dhal or split peas in 1 litre/ 32 fl oz/4 cups of boiling water for 40 minutes or until soft.

Heat the ghee or oil in a wok, add the ginger garlic paste and cook for 5 minutes. Add the tomato purée and cook over a high heat for 10 minutes, or until the sauce becomes thick and dry.

Add the spices and salt to the wok and cook them for 2 minutes. Stir in the cream and split peas and simmer for 5 minutes, or until heated through.

sour vegetable and egg curry

Sour curries are among the most popular of all Thai curries. They have a soupy consistency and are best eaten with steamed jasmine rice. The sourness comes from the tamarind concentrate, which can be bought in Asian food stores.

Preparation time: 15 minutes,
cooking time: 20 minutes, serves 4–6

750 ml/24 fl oz/generous 3 cups vegetable stock
2 tablespoons tamarind concentrate
2 teaspoons grated palm sugar or brown sugar
2 tablespoons red curry paste
6 hard-boiled eggs, peeled
225 g/8 oz can bamboo shoots, drained
200 g/7 oz shiitake mushrooms, halved
2 cucumbers, cut into bite-size pieces
2 tomatoes, cut into wedges
125 g/4½ oz shredded Chinese cabbage

Heat the stock, tamarind, sugar and red curry paste in a large pan, bring it to the boil, then reduce the heat to a simmer. Add the eggs and vegetables and cook for 15 minutes, or until the vegetables are soft.

dhal makhan

sour vegetable and egg curry

potato masala

This potato mixture is the filling that is contained within the wafer-thin crisp dosa that are enjoyed for breakfast, lunch, dinner and snacks in India. I love it just on its own, but try it with some warm chapattis and coconut chutney (see page 154).

Preparation time: 10 minutes,
cooking time: 30 minutes, serves 4–6

500 g/1 lb 2 oz potatoes
3 tablespoons vegetable oil
½ teaspoon black mustard seeds
10 curry leaves
1–2 small green chillies, seeded and chopped
1 red onion, chopped
½ teaspoon turmeric
½ teaspoon salt

Peel the potatoes and cook them in a large pan of boiling water for 10 minutes, or until they are just turning soft. Drain them well and allow them to cool slightly before roughly chopping them.

Heat the oil in a pan, add the mustard seeds and cook them over a medium heat for 3 minutes, or until they pop. Add the curry leaves, chillies and onion and cook them for 10 minutes, or until the onion are golden.

Add the turmeric, potatoes, 2 tablespoons of water and salt to the pan and cook for 5 minutes, or until heated through.

pagara bengan

This recipe name, directly translated, is 'seasoned aubergine/eggplant'. Originating in Hyberabad, this is perhaps one of my all-time favourite vegetable curries. It is very rich and should be served with bread or alongside biryani.

Preparation time: 20 minutes,
cooking time: 50 minutes, serves 4–6

8 small aubergines (eggplants)
1 tablespoon desiccated (dry unsweetened) coconut
1 tablespoon coriander seeds
1 tablespoon sesame seeds
2 teaspoons ground cumin
2 tablespoons raw peanuts
½ teaspoon hot chilli powder
½ teaspoon garam masala
½ teaspoon fennel seeds
1 teaspoon tamarind concentrate
2 cm/¾ inch piece ginger, peeled
3 garlic cloves
4 tablespoons vegetable oil
½ teaspoon salt
1 teaspoon grated palm sugar or brown sugar

Cut the aubergines almost in half, taking care not to cut all the way through, and leaving the stalks on.

Roast the coconut, coriander, sesame seeds, cumin and peanuts in a nonstick pan or wok for 3–5 minutes. Allow to cool and transfer to a food processor or spice grinder, add the chilli powder, garam masala, fennel, tamarind, ginger and garlic and grind to form a paste. You may have to add a few tablespoons of water in order to bring the mixture together.

Heat the oil in a wok, add the aubergines (eggplants) and cook them for 3 minutes, or until the skins soften. Add the spice mix and cook until the paste forms a ball.

Add 250 ml/9 fl oz/1 cup of water to the wok, bring it to the boil, reduce the heat and simmer, covered, for 30 minutes, or until the aubergines are soft.

Remove the lid from the wok, add the salt and sugar and cook for 10 minutes, or until the oil separates from the sauce mixture.

potato masala

pagara bengan

aunty's mysore dhal

aunty's mysore dhal

This simple dhal recipe was given to me by my friend Aunty at one of the many cooking classes I did with her in Mysore while researching this book. If you are unable to find choko/chayote, you can use courgette (zucchini) instead.

Preparation time: 10 minutes, cooking time: 1 hour, serves 4–6

200 g/7 oz/1 cup yellow split peas
¼ teaspoon turmeric
1 teaspoon vegetable oil
1 choko, peeled and finely chopped
1 teaspoon salt
22 g/¾ oz/¼ cup grated coconut or desiccated (dry unsweetened) coconut
2 teaspoons lemon juice

Boil the split peas and turmeric in 1 litre/ 32 fl oz/4 cups water along with the oil for 45 minutes, or until the peas are tender. Add the choko and salt and simmer for 10 minutes, or until the choko is soft. Add the coconut and lemon juice and cook for 2 minutes, or until heated through.

coconut, chickpea and vegetable curry

The English created curry powder in the 17th century after returning from India, as it provided them with a quick and easy way of making curries without all the roasting and grinding of spices.

Preparation time: 20 minutes, cooking time: 50 minutes, serves 4–6

2 tablespoons vegetable oil
1 onion, chopped
3 tablespoons curry powder
6 baby potatoes, halved
2 carrots, sliced
4 baby aubergines (eggplants) sliced
300 g/10½ oz cauliflower florets
400 g/14 oz can chickpeas, rinsed and drained
400 ml/14 fl oz/1¾ cups coconut milk
2 tomatoes, chopped
1 teaspoon grated palm sugar or brown sugar
½ teaspoon salt

Heat the oil in a pan, add the onion and cook over a medium heat for 10 minutes, or until golden. Add the curry powder and cook for 2 minutes, or until fragrant.

Add the vegetables, chickpeas, coconut milk, tomatoes, 250 ml/9 fl oz/1 cup of water, sugar and salt to the pan, then cover and simmer for 30 minutes. Remove the lid and cook for a further 5 minutes, or until the sauce thickens slightly.

coconut, chickpea and vegetable curry

avial

Avial is a vegetable curry from Kerala and most people use whatever vegetables are available in it. For a stronger coconut flavour, toast the coconut in a dry frying pan before grinding it with the other spices.

Preparation time: 15 minutes, cooking time: 25–30 minutes, serves 4–6

45 g/1½ oz/½ cup desiccated (dry unsweetened) coconut
1 teaspoon coriander seeds
3 garlic cloves
1 red onion, chopped
2 large dried red chillies, broken
¼ teaspoon turmeric
1 teaspoon tamarind concentrate
2 tablespoons vegetable oil
10 okra, halved
100 g/3½ oz green beans, sliced
125 g/4½ oz cauliflower florets
80 g/2¾ oz/generous ¾ cup green peas
2 potatoes, cubed
1 carrot, diced

Put the coconut, coriander, garlic, onion, chillies, turmeric and tamarind into a food processor and process to form a paste – you may need to add some water to bring the paste together.

Heat the oil in a pan, add the okra and cook it for 5 minutes or until soft and brown. Add the remaining vegetables and 1 cup (250 ml/8 fl oz) of water, cover and cook for 10 minutes.

Add the spice paste to the pan, cover and cook for 10 minutes or until the vegetables are soft.

red vegetable and pineapple curry

This is a traditional quick and easy curry that can be made using any fruit and vegetables you have available in your refrigerator. For example, you could substitute the pineapple with mango or banana.

Preparation time: 15 minutes, cooking time: 20 minutes, serves 4–6

1 tablespoon vegetable oil
1 tablespoon red curry paste
500 ml/18 fl oz coconut milk/generous 2 cups (including the cream)
1 carrot, sliced
1 red pepper (bell pepper), sliced
200 g/7 oz cauliflower, cut into florets
1 tablespoon lime juice
1 tablespoon grated palm sugar or brown sugar
200 g/7 oz broccoli, cut into florets
100 g/3½ oz mangetout (snow peas)
400 g/14 oz fresh pineapple, cut into small pieces
2 tablespoons finely shredded kaffir limes, to serve

Heat the oil in a wok, add the curry paste and the thick coconut cream from the top of a can of coconut milk to the wok and cook over a medium heat, stirring occasionally, for 3 minutes, or until the oil starts to separate from the cream.

Add the coconut milk, carrot, red pepper, cauliflower, lime juice and sugar to the pan and bring the mixture to the boil, then reduce the heat and simmer for 10 minutes.

Add the broccoli, mangetout and pineapple and simmer for 5 minutes, or until the broccoli is tender. Serve sprinkled with the shredded kaffir lime leaves.

red vegetable and pineapple curry

green vegetable and tofu curry

Any vegetarian who has ever travelled to Thailand will have an intimate relationship with green vegetable and tofu curry. There are never two the same, as there are endless possibilities for different vegetable combinations.

Preparation time: 20 minutes, cooking time: 30 minutes, serves 4–6

1 tablespoon vegetable oil
1–2 tablespoons green curry paste
500 ml/18 fl oz/generous 2 cups coconut cream
300 g/10½ oz pumpkin, cut into large pieces
200 g/7 oz snake beans or green beans
100 g/3½ oz fresh or canned baby corn
100 g/3½ oz shiitake mushrooms
2 tomatoes, cut into wedges
250 g/9 oz firm tofu, cubed
1 tablespoon Thai fish sauce (optional)
1 tablespoon grated palm sugar or brown sugar

Heat the oil in a wok, add the curry paste and stir-fry over a medium heat with 60 ml/ 2 fl oz/¼ cup hot water until the water boils and the curry paste is fragrant.

Add the coconut cream, pumpkin, snake beans, corn, mushrooms, tomatoes, tofu, fish sauce (if using) and sugar, bring to the boil, then reduce the heat and simmer for 20 minutes, or until the pumpkin is tender.

satay tofu curry sticks

These are delicious cooked on the barbecue (grill). Obviously the longer the tofu stays in the marinade, the more flavour it will absorb.

Preparation time: 20 minutes + 20 minutes soaking and 30 minutes marinating, cooking time: 15–20 minutes, serves 4–6

4 large dried red chillies
2 garlic cloves
½ teaspoon salt
150 g/5½ oz/1 cup roasted peanuts
1 tablespoon vegetable oil
250 ml/9 fl oz/1 cup coconut milk
1 teaspoon grated palm sugar or brown sugar
1 teaspoon white vinegar
750 g/1 lb 10 oz firm tofu, cut into 5 cm/2 inch pieces
2 tablespoons soy sauce
2 tablespoons sweet chilli sauce
6 spring onions (scallions), cut into 5 cm/2 inch pieces
2 tablespoons vegetable oil

Soak some bamboo skewers in cold water for 20 minutes to prevent them burning when they are placed on the barbecue (grill).

To make the satay, soak the chillies in hot water for 15 minutes, or until soft, then drain them well and roughly chop them. Put the chillies into a food processor, add the garlic, salt and peanuts and process until smooth.

Heat the oil in a pan, add the paste and cook over a medium heat for 5 minutes, or until fragrant. Add the coconut milk, sugar and vinegar and simmer for 5–10 minutes, or until the oil comes to the surface.

Marinate the tofu pieces in the soy and sweet chilli sauce for a minimum of 30 minutes.

Thread the tofu and spring onions onto the bamboo skewers, then cook them on a lightly oiled barbecue (grill) or in a frying pan for 5 minutes, or until golden brown all over. Serve with the satay sauce.

sticky red tempeh curry

Tempeh is made by pressing and fermenting soya beans into edible steaks. It can be purchased in health food stores, but if it is not available use firm tofu as an alternative.

Preparation time: 20 minutes, cooking time: 20 minutes, serves 4–6

300 g/10½ oz tempeh, cut into thin strips
groundnut (peanut) oil, for deep frying
1 large red chilli, seeded and thinly sliced
1 tablespoon red curry paste
2 tablespoons tamarind concentrate
4 tablespoons fried shallots
4 tablespoons grated palm sugar or brown sugar
1 carrot, sliced
1 red pepper (bell pepper), sliced
2 tablespoons fresh coriander (cilantro) leaves

Deep-fry the tempeh in the oil for 3–5 minutes, or until crisp and golden brown, then drain on absorbent kitchen paper.

Heat 1 tablespoon of the oil that was used for deep-frying in a wok, add the chilli and curry paste and stir fry over a medium heat for 3 minutes, or until fragrant.

Add the tamarind, fried shallots and sugar to the wok and stir until the sugar dissolves. Add 60 ml/2 fl oz/¼ cup of water and bring the mixture to the boil, then cook for 5 minutes, or until sticky.

Add the carrot and red pepper and cook until soft. Finally, add the tempeh and coriander and cook until heated through.

satay tofu curry sticks

sticky red tempeh curry

spinach dhal

No Indian meal is complete without a bowl of dhal. The addition of spinach to this recipe makes it feel more like a main meal than a side dish, though – teamed with some warm roti, it makes a wonderfully satisfying evening meal.

Preparation time: 15 minutes,
cooking time: 1 hour, serves 4–6

200 g/7 oz/1 cup moong dhal or yellow split peas
500 g/1 lb 2 oz English spinach, trimmed and chopped
¼ teaspoon asafoetida
¼ teaspoon turmeric
½ teaspoon salt
2 tablespoons vegetable oil
1 teaspoon black mustard seeds
1 teaspoon cumin seeds
10 curry leaves
¼ teaspoon paprika
2 garlic cloves, thinly sliced

Cook the dhal or split peas in a pan with 750 ml/24 fl oz/generous 3 cups of water, covered, for 45 minutes, or until soft. Add the spinach, asafoetida, turmeric and salt and cook for 10 minutes, or until the spinach is soft and the mixture is thick.

Heat the oil in a pan, then add the mustard and cumin seeds and cook over a medium heat for 3 minutes, or until the mustard seeds pop. Add the curry leaves, paprika and garlic and cook for 2 minutes.

Spoon the dhal into a bowl and pour the spiced oil over the top.

dum aloo

Dum means to steam or cook anything covered, while aloo is a north Indian term for potatoes. (Potatoes are a staple of the Indian diet.) This dish would traditionally have Kashmiri chillies in it to give it its colour.

Preparation time: 15 minutes + 15 minutes
soaking, cooking time: 50 minutes, serves 4–6

4 large dried red chillies
1 red onion, chopped
3 garlic cloves, chopped
1 teaspoon garam masala
½ teaspoon turmeric
3 tablespoons vegetable oil
1 kg/2 lb 4 oz baby potatoes
125 g/4 ½ oz/½ cup natural (plain) yoghurt
1 teaspoon salt
1 teaspoon sugar

Soak the chillies in boiling water for 15 minutes, then drain them. Put the chillies, onion, garlic, garam masala and turmeric into a food processor and process until smooth – you may need to add a little water in order to bring the mixture together.

Heat the oil in a pan, add the spice paste and cook it over a medium heat for 10 minutes, or until the oil separates from the paste.

Add the potatoes and 250 ml/9 fl oz/1 cup of water into the pan, cover and cook for 20 minutes, or until the potato is soft. Remove the lid and simmer for a further 10 minutes or until the sauce thickens slightly. Finally, add the yoghurt, salt and sugar and simmer for 1 minute, or until heated through.

spinach dhal

dum aloo

mustard mango curry

mustard mango curry

This delicious curry is a welcome addition to a spicy meal. Traditionally, mango is eaten in the middle of the day, as Indians believe that it is a difficult fruit to digest; I have included ginger in this recipe to help aid its digestion.

Preparation time: 15 minutes, cooking time: 15 minutes, serves 4–6

90 g/3 oz/1 cup desiccated (dry unsweetened) coconut
1 tablespoon grated fresh ginger
¼ teaspoon turmeric
½ teaspoon hot chilli powder
6 black peppercorns
1 teaspoon tamarind concentrate
1 tablespoon vegetable oil
1 teaspoon black mustard seeds
6 curry leaves
½ teaspoon salt
3 mangoes, cut into thick slices

Put the coconut, ginger, turmeric, hot chilli powder, peppercorns and tamarind into a food processor and process to form a smooth paste – you may need to add some water to bring the mixture together.

Heat the oil in a pan, add the mustard seeds and cook over a medium heat for 3 minutes, or until they begin to pop. Add the curry leaves, coconut paste and salt and cook until the oil separates from the sauce.

Add the mangoes and 125 ml/4 fl oz/½ cup of water to the pan and gently mix to combine the ingredients. Simmer for 3 minutes, or until heated through.

gujarati sweet sour vegetable curry

Gujarat is a state in the west of India and the food there tends to be spicy, sweet and dry. If you would like a little extra gravy, add more water or tomatoes towards the end of cooking (if you use the latter, balance the flavour with extra sugar).

Preparation time: 20 minutes, cooking time: 30 minutes, serves 4–6

250 g/9 oz orange sweet potatoes, peeled and cubed
250 g/9 oz cauliflower, cut into florets
1 teaspoon salt
1 teaspoon hot chilli powder
½ teaspoon turmeric
1 teaspoon ground coriander
1 teaspoon ground cumin
3 tablespoons vegetable oil
8 curry leaves
1 tablespoon tamarind concentrate
200 g/7 oz ripe tomatoes, chopped
1 tablespoon grated palm sugar or brown sugar

Put the sweet potato and cauliflower into a bowl, then add the spices and 1 tablespoon water and mix to coat the vegetables in the spice mix.

Heat the oil in a pan, add the vegetables and cook for 5 minutes, or until golden. Add the curry leaves, tamarind, 250 ml/9 fl oz/1 cup of water, the tomatoes and sugar, then simmer uncovered for 20 minutes, or until the vegetables are soft and the sauce is thick.

gujarati sweet sour vegetable curry

palak paneer

This is a favourite Punjabi dish and it can be made even more decadent by finishing it with a few generous dollops of melted ghee. Paneer can be purchased in Indian food stores, but can be substituted with firm tofu if you can't find it.

Preparation time: 15 minutes,
cooking time: 25 minutes, serves 4–6

2 red onions, chopped
1 garlic clove
3 small green chillies
2 cm/¾ inch piece ginger, peeled
3 tablespoons vegetable oil
125 g/4¼ oz paneer, cubed
500 g/1 lb 2 oz/2 bunches English spinach, trimmed
1 teaspoon cornflour (cornstarch)
2 tablespoons ghee or butter
1 teaspoon ground cumin
½ teaspoon garam masala
55 g/2 oz/¼ cup natural (plain) yoghurt
½ teaspoon salt
1 tablespoon single (light) cream

Put the onions, garlic, chillies and ginger into a food processor and process until smooth – you may need to add a little water to make a smooth paste. Heat the oil in a pan, add the paneer and cook it for 3–5 minutes, until golden. Remove it from the pan and drain on absorbent kitchen paper.

Rinse the spinach and cook it, covered, in a pan, for 5 minutes, or until it wilts. Transfer it to a food processor, add the cornflour and process until smooth and creamy.

Heat the ghee in a pan, add the cumin and garam masala and cook for 2 minutes, or until fragrant. Add the onion-chilli paste and cook for a further 10 minutes, or until the oil separates from the sauce. Stir in the yoghurt and cook until thick and dry. Add the spinach purée, salt, cream and paneer to the pan, bring to the boil and cook for 2 minutes.

moong dhal

Moong dhal is available in Indian food stores. If you cannot buy it, yellow split peas will work well but may not be as creamy. (If using split peas, you may need to simmer the dhal for a little longer to evaporate any excess water.)

Preparation time: 15 minutes,
cooking time: 1 hour, serves 4–6

400 g/14 oz/2 cups moong dhal or yellow split peas
2 tablespoons vegetable oil
2 teaspoons black mustard seeds
2 teaspoons ground coriander
2 teaspoons ground cumin
½ teaspoon hot chilli powder
5 cloves
1 cinnamon stick
10 curry leaves
3 ripe tomatoes, chopped
1 tablespoon grated palm sugar or brown sugar
1 tablespoon tamarind concentrate
poppadoms, to serve

Cook the dhal or split peas in 1 litre/32 fl oz/ 4 cups of water for 45 minutes, or until soft.

Heat the oil in a pan, add the mustard seeds and cook over a medium heat for 3 minutes, or until they begin to pop. Add the spices and cook for 3 minutes, or until fragrant. Add the tomatoes, sugar and tamarind and cook for 5–10 minutes, or until thick and dry.

Stir in the dhal and cook for 5 minutes or until heated through, then serve it with poppadoms.

palak paneer

moong dhal

bean thoren

bean thoren

This is another very simple dry vegetable curry originating in south India. For an alternative, try using spinach or aubergine (eggplant) instead of the beans.

Preparation time: 10 minutes,
cooking time: 20 minutes, serves 4–6

2 tablespoons vegetable oil
1 teaspoon black mustard seeds
2 dried red chillies, torn or cut into large pieces
2 teaspoons curry powder
8 curry leaves
500 g/1 lb 2 oz green beans, sliced
½ teaspoon salt
2 teaspoons grated palm sugar or brown sugar

Heat the oil in a pan, add the mustard seeds and cook over a medium heat for 3 minutes, or until they begin to pop. Add the chillies and cook for 2 minutes.

Add the curry powder, curry leaves, beans, salt and 2 tablespoons of water to the pan and simmer, uncovered, for 5–10 minutes, or until the beans are soft. Add the sugar and cook for 5 minutes, or until heated through.

simple vegetable curry

This is a quick and easy recipe for those of you who don't want to spend time making pastes. There are a number of good-quality ones now available in shops. I have chosen a Madras paste – you could use a milder tandoori or korma paste.

Preparation time: 15 minutes,
cooking time: 50 minutes, serves 4–6

2 tablespoons vegetable oil
1 red onion, finely chopped
2 tablespoons Madras curry paste
1 carrot, thickly sliced
300 g/10½ oz pumpkin, cut into cubes
2 courgettes (zucchini), sliced
1 green pepper (bell pepper), chopped
150 g/5½ oz/1½ cups peas
400 g/14 oz can chopped tomatoes
125 ml/4 fl oz/½ cup natural (plain) yoghurt
40 g/1½ oz/scant ¼ cup cashews, to serve

Heat the oil in a pan, add the onion and cook over a medium heat for 10 minutes, or until caramelized. Add the curry paste and cook for 3 minutes, or until the oil separates from the paste.

Add the vegetables, tomatoes and 250 ml/ 9 fl oz/1 cup of water and simmer, covered, for 20 minutes. Remove the lid and simmer for a further 15 minutes, or until the vegetables are soft. Remove the pan from the heat and stir in the yoghurt. Serve sprinkled with the cashews.

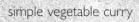
simple vegetable curry

pastes, condiments and rice

masaman curry paste

Roast 3 bruised cardamom pods, 1 teaspoon cumin seeds, 1 tablespoon coriander seeds, 5 cloves and 1 sheath of mace in a frying pan for 3 minutes, or until fragrant, then grind in a mortar and pestle or food processor to a fine powder. Sift the spices to remove any fibrous husks. Split 6 large dried red chillies down their centres and remove the seeds and white membranes (this is best done while wearing plastic gloves). Soak the chillies in cold water for 15 minutes, then drain and pat dry. Place the chillies, 1 teaspoon of salt, 1 tablespoon of chopped galangal (optional), 2 tablespoons of chopped lemongrass, 2 teaspoons of coriander root, 3 tablespoons of chopped Asian shallots, 4 tablespoons of chopped garlic and 2 tablespoons of chopped roasted peanuts, along with the spice mixture, to the mortar and pestle or food processor and process until finely ground. Store the paste in an airtight container in the refrigerator or freeze it for up to 2 months. *Makes 250 g/9 oz/1 cup.*

green curry paste

Roast ½ teaspoon each of cumin and coriander seeds in a frying pan for 3 minutes, or until fragrant, then transfer to a food processor along with 1 teaspoon of white peppercorns and 1 teaspoon of turmeric. Process to form a fine powder. Add 12 seeded and roughly chopped large green chillies and 1 teaspoon of salt and process until finely ground. Next add 2 teaspoons of chopped galangal (optional) and grind until it has been incorporated into the chillies. Add 4 chopped stalks of lemongrass, 1 tablespoon of chopped coriander root, 3 tablespoons of chopped Asian shallots, 2 tablespoons of chopped garlic and 1 teaspoon of shrimp paste and process until you form a smooth paste. Store in an airtight container in the refrigerator or freeze for up to 2 months. *Makes 250 g/9 oz/1 cup.*

red curry paste

Split 10 large dried red chillies down their centres and remove the seeds and white membranes (wear plastic gloves while you do this). Soak the chillies in cold water for 15 minutes, then drain and pat dry. Put the chillies along with 1 teaspoon of salt into a food processor or mortar and pestle and process until finely ground. Add 1 teaspoon of chopped galangal (optional), 2 tablespoons of chopped lemongrass and process until smooth. Add 1 teaspoon of grated kaffir lime rind, 4 tablespoons of chopped Asian shallots, 1 teaspoon of chopped coriander root, 2 tablespoons of chopped garlic and 1 teaspoon of shrimp paste and process or grind until smooth. Store in an airtight container in the refrigerator or freeze for up to 2 months. *Makes 250 g/9 oz/1 cup.*

garam masala

Garam masala is a basic, easy-to-remember recipe, as it contains equal quantities of cinnamon, cloves, pepper and a small amount of cardamom. Any excess can be stored in an airtight container in the refrigerator. To make the spice mix used for the recipes in this book, put 2 cinnamon sticks and 2 teaspoons each of cloves, black peppercorns, fennel seeds, cardamom pods and 2 bay leaves into a spice grinder or food processor and process to fine powder. *Makes 55 g/2 oz/⅓ cup.*

ginger garlic paste

Used extensively in Indian curries, this is a good paste to make ahead of time and store in the refrigerator in an airtight container for up to 5 days. Put 100 g/3½ oz/½ cup of grated ginger and 70 g/2¼ oz/½ cup of peeled garlic cloves into a food processor or mortar and pestle and grind until you have a smooth paste. *Makes 165 g/5¾ oz/¾ cup.*

masaman curry paste

green curry paste

red curry paste

garam masala

ginger garlic paste

coriander (cilantro) mint chutney

This chutney goes particularly well with meat dishes. Put 1 cup each of fresh mint and coriander (cilantro) leaves into a food processor. Add 1 chopped small green chilli, ½ chopped small red onion, ½ teaspoon each of chopped garlic, ginger, ground cumin and salt. Add 1 teaspoon sugar, 1 tablespoon lime juice and process until roughly chopped. Store in an airtight container in the refrigerator for up to a week. *Makes 500 g/1 lb 2 oz/2 cups.*
∗ You may want to add 3 tablespoons of natural (plain) yoghurt as a variation.

banana, coconut and coriander (cilantro)

This is a fantastic accompaniment to spicy meat curries. The bananas should be ripe but firm. It is delicious if made with sugar or lady finger bananas, which are widely available in Asia. If you can get them, double the amount of bananas you use, as they are quite small. The recipe is also good with natural (plain) yoghurt folded through it. (You may also like to add some sultanas/golden raisins and chopped dried apricots.) It is best made just before serving. Cut 3 bananas into thick slices and place in a bowl, then drizzle over 1 tablespoon of lime juice and gently mix to combine. Fold through 20 g/¾ oz/¼ cup of desiccated (dry unsweetened) coconut and 1 tablespoon of chopped fresh coriander (cilantro). *Makes 500 g/ 1 lb 2 oz/2 cups.*

coconut chutney

Served with Indian curries, this chutney can be made a day in advance. It is best made with fresh coconut, but if you are short on time you can use 90 g/3¼ oz/1 cup of desiccated (dry unsweetened) coconut instead. Remove the flesh from 1 coconut, taking off any skin with a knife. Put the coconut into a food processor and chop finely. Add 3 chopped small green chillies, 1 tablespoon of grated fresh ginger and 3 tablespoons of water and process until well combined. Transfer the mixture to a bowl. Heat 1 tablespoon of vegetable oil in a pan, then add 1 teaspoon of black mustard seeds and cook over a medium heat for 2–3 minutes, or until they start to pop. Add 10 curry leaves and cook for 2 minutes, or until fragrant. Add to the coconut mixture and mix well. Store in an airtight container in the refrigerator for up to 2 weeks. *Makes 500 g/1 lb 2 oz/2 cups.*

tomato and onion cachumber

Mexicans eat their meals with a salsa, while Indians team their meals with a cachumber. It is very similar – salad made with raw vegetables that accompanies a meal. To make this cachumber, put 2 diced tomatoes and 1 diced small red onion into a bowl, add 1 tablespoon of chopped fresh coriander (cilantro), 2 teaspoons of lime juice and a pinch of sea salt, then gently mix to combine. *Makes 500 g/1 lb 2 oz/2 cups.*

reena's tomato date chutney

I first ate this chutney with chapatti in my instructor Reena's backyard one morning before a cooking class. The combination of the sweetness of the dates combined with aromatic fennel is quite unique. Serve it as part of a meal or, as Reena did, with Indian bread. To make the chutney, heat 1 tablespoon of vegetable oil in a pan and add 1 teaspoon each of black mustard seeds, fenugreek seeds and fennel seeds and fry until the mustard seeds pop. Add 1 kg/2 lb 4 oz of chopped ripe tomatoes and cook these over a medium heat until soft. Then add generous 55 g/2 oz/⅓ cup of raisins, 200 g/7 oz/ 1 cup of grated palm sugar (or brown sugar), 175 g/6 oz/1 cup of dates, 2 tablespoons of white vinegar and 1 teaspoon of salt. Simmer for 40 minutes, or until the mixture is thick, then spoon it into sterilized jars. It can be stored for up to a month. *Makes 1–1.5 kg/2–3 lb/4–6 cups.*

coriander (cilantro) mint chutney

banana, coconut and coriander

coconut chutney

tomato and onion cachumber

reena's tomato date chutney

saffron rice

This is a fairly classic Indian rice. I simply adore the subtle saffron aroma and I think it can be served with most Indian curries. Saffron powder does not have the same flavour and should not be used as a substitute for saffron threads. Soak ½ teaspoon of saffron threads in 2 tablespoons of warm milk for 10 minutes. Rinse 350 g/12 oz/1¾ cups of basmati rice under cold running water, then transfer the rice and saffron and milk mixture to a large pan. Add 1 tablespoon of ghee, 1 cinnamon stick, 1 teaspoon of salt and 850 ml/28 fl oz/3¾ cups of water and bring the mixture to the boil. Cook it over a high heat until tunnels form in the rice. Cover the pan and cook it over a low heat for 15 minutes without removing the lid, or until the rice is soft and all the liquid has been absorbed. *Serves 4–6.*

cooling cucumber raita

Indians eat raita with curries, as it is cooling and makes the perfect accompaniment to a spicy curry. It is quick and easy to make and can be as simple as yoghurt seasoned with a little salt, pepper and ground cumin. To make this raita, put 1 diced Lebanese cucumber into a bowl, add ½ diced red onion, 250 g/9 oz/1 cup of natural (plain) yoghurt, ¼ teaspoon each of ground cumin, paprika, salt and sugar and 1 teaspoon of chopped fresh coriander (cilantro). Mix to combine all the ingredients. *Makes 500 g/ 1lb 2 oz/2 cups.*

lemon rice

This rice goes well with mild Indian curries. Rinse 350 g/12 oz/1¾ cups of basmati rice in a colander. Transfer it to a large saucepan, add 850 ml/28 fl oz/ 3¾ cups of water, 55 g/2 oz/½ cup of sultanas (golden raisins), 1 bruised cardamom pod, ¼ teaspoon of turmeric and 1 tablespoon of ghee and bring the mixture to the boil. Cook it over a high heat until tunnels form in the rice, then cover and cook over a low heat for 15 minutes, or until the rice is soft and all the liquid has been absorbed. Fold through 2 tablespoons of lemon juice and 50 g/1¾ oz/⅓ cup roasted cashews. *Serves 4–6.*

ginger yoghurt

This is a great palate cleanser for hotter curries. To make it, put 250 g/9 oz/1 cup of natural (plain) yoghurt into a bowl, add 1 tablespoon of grated fresh ginger, ½ teaspoon each of finely diced small green chilli, salt and grated palm sugar (or brown sugar) and mix to combine. *Makes 500 g/1 lb 2 oz/2 cups.*

yoghurt rice

This is so simple, but I had to include it as I was so impressed by the way it can transform a meal. I first ate this at Aunty's restaurant in Mysore with a spicy vegetable curry and dhal. It is especially delicious with dry curries such as the mussel and squid fry (see page 108). To make it, rinse 350 g/12 oz/1¾ cups of basmati rice in a colander. Transfer to a large saucepan, add 850 ml/28 fl oz/3¾ cups of water and bring to the boil. Cook over a high heat until tunnels form in the rice, then cover and cook over a low heat for 15 minutes, or until the rice is soft and all the liquid has been absorbed. Finally, fold through 250 g/9 oz/1 cup of natural (plain) yoghurt before serving. *Serves 4–6.*

saffron rice

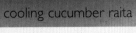

cooling cucumber raita

lemon rice

ginger yoghurt

yoghurt rice

index

Author and stylist Jody Vassallo
Home economist Michelle Lucia
Recipe testing Abi Ulgati
Props stylists Carlu Seavers and Melissa Singer
Photographer Deirdre Rooney

Publisher Catie Ziller
Project editor Claire Musters
Art director Deirdre Rooney

Props credits We would like to thank the following companies: Accountrement, Bed, Bath and Table, Design Mode International, Food Stuff Monavale, Travellers and Traders, Village Living and Wheel and Barrow Homewares.

The publisher would also like to thank Sunbeam Appliances, Australia for all the woks and food processor used to cook the recipes in this book.

Author acknowledgements Firstly, I would like to thank Catie Ziller for yet again providing me with the opportunity to do what I love most – make gorgeous cookbooks. It was wonderful to travel around India and attend daily cooking classes with awe-inspiring women; this book would not have been possible without the information I received from my magnificent cooking instructors – Usha Kotak, Reena, Teena and Aunty.

Thanks to Fish; you never balked at anything I wanted to try and never tired of helping me shop for props. To Claire Musters, who left no curry unchecked – your watchful eye is so appreciated. To Deirdre Rooney, thank you for bringing out the best in my work. Michelle Lucia, thank you for giving it your heart and soul. Abi, thanks for 'yumming' day in, day out and always coming back for yet another little spoonful. Carlu Seaver, I thank you for your dedication and stylish eye that enabled this book to look as beautiful as it does, and Mel Singer, thanks for zipping around in search of 'the' fabric. And thanks to all my friends, family and guinea pigs who endured week after week of curries, faithfully returning the plastic containers and providing encouraging feedback.

To Pridey Joy, cheeky dog wonder (who doesn't really have a thing for curries) for loving me, challenging me and making me laugh.

Lastly, I would like to thank all the wonderful people I have encountered on my trips to Thailand and India for embracing me with a hospitality that is sometimes forgotten in the Western world.

I would like to dedicate this book to my dear smiling friend Jem, who liked it spicy! I wish you could have been here to try some – hope you got some of the lovely smells way up there.

© Marabout (Hachette Livre), 2004
This edition published by Hachette Illustrated UK,
Octopus Publishing Group Ltd., 2–4 Heron Quays, London E14 4JP

Additional editorial work by JMS Books LLP (email: moseleystrachan@aol.com)
Translation © Octopus Publishing Group Ltd.

A CIP catalogue for this book is available from the British Library

ISBN-13: 978-1-84430-102-7

ISBN-10: 1-84430-102-8

Printed by Toppan Printing Co., (HK) Ltd.